D1152817

RIVERSIDE RAMBLES
along
THE MERSEY

Ron Freethy

Published by Sigma Leisure – an imprint of
Sigma Press, 5 Alton Road, Wilmslow, Cheshire SK9 5DY, England.

British Library Cataloguing in Publication Data
A CIP record for this book is available from the British Library.

ISBN: 1-85058-812-0

Typesetting and Design by: Sigma Press, Wilmslow, Cheshire.

Cover: postcard of the Mersey; Cadbury's advertisement ca. 1909

Maps: © Ron Freethy 2004. Produced by Gelder Design & Mapping from sketches declared by the author to be based on original research.

Printed by: Interprint Ltd, Malta

FOREWORD

By David Bellamy OBE

At the heart of every living landscape is, or rather was, a living river. When I was young it was a place where families walked and children played, learning to swim while coming face to face with adventure and the challenge of natural history. School trips took you to the water works from which pure water flowed into our homes, and to the sewage works where that same water was cleaned up and made useable once again. Since those 'Wind in the Willows' days, the winds of change have blown in many directions, from muck and luck and muck and brass, to integrated catchment management, and towards sustainability and beyond.

The Mersey is one such river, made famous by its manufactories and docks; the gateway to the New World long before The Beatles and The Scaffold said their thank you's to the angle iron.

Though canalised in parts and grotesquely polluted in the past, recent years have seen dramatic improvements audited by the return of wildlife from its source to its ever-changing estuary.

What better person to introduce the history, both natural and man made, of this living legend of a river, than an ecologist and journalist who has spend over 30 years travelling the world reporting on the problems and potentials of putting rivers back into more natural working order? And what better way of doing it than through his eyes, ears and expertise to guide you on 30 short gentle walks?

If you love the Mersey buy this book and take those walks, soaking up the knowledge and the wonder of this once-again living river. Ron Freethy, thank you very much for the angle on this story – thank you very, very, very much.

David Bellamy, Bedburn

PREFACE

In 1983, I was asked to write a series of hour-long documentaries for Granada Television about the rivers of England. I decided to start with the Mersey, which was then heavily polluted. My brief was to look not only for so called 'black spots' but also to concentrate upon areas which were still delightful and which could still attract tourists. Then came the Toxteth riots and Michael Heseltine, working under Margaret Thatcher, visited the Mersey and said that the condition of the river was "an affront to a civilised society".

In 1985, the government set up the Mersey Basin Campaign set to run until 2010 and with the brief of improving the river. As journalist and ecologist, I have been involved with the Campaign since its inception until 2002 and I am delighted that it has achieved many of its objectives. In 1999, the Campaign won the inaugural Riverprize for the best river clean-up in the world. The prize was awarded in Brisbane, Australia and I was pleased to accept this award on behalf of the Campaign. To the present day, I have been an honorary director of the International Riverprize board.

In the course of all my work on the Mersey and its tributaries, I have walked many miles along its banks. Many of the Mersey's tributaries are linked into an intricate canal system and these have also been the subject of major improvements. This present book is a selection of gentle walks along these watercourses. It maps out the ecological improvements, industrial archaeology, tourist attractions and geographical features. Most of the walks are circular but a few linear walks have been described – though these are always linked to at least one mode of public transport.

Two future developments will change the Mersey for the better. Firstly, a new vehicular crossing is planned in the Widnes area. Secondly, Liverpool's selection as the European City of Culture for 2008 will focus attention on the whole area and the Mersey is well placed to play a major role. Indeed, whenever river catchment systems are mentioned nowadays, the Mersey is one of the first to be mentioned – what a contrast to the days when we filmed the Granada documentary! I am proud to have played a bit part in the Mersey's soap opera. The Mucky Mersey should now be renamed the Mighty Mersey.

Ron Freethy

Acknowledgements

It is quite right to say that any errors within these pages are the responsibility of the author. It is also right, however, that those who have helped in its preparation should be mentioned.

I thank Keith Hall for his continued encouragement during my riverside rambles. I also thank him for showing me the old postcard which graces the front cover of the book.

Graham Veevers and the staff of the East Lancashire Railway provided essential details of the line; they also make a good brew of tea. This was also the case when I visited the Roman Lakes Country Park, surely one of the best 'free' amenities to be found along the Mersey catchment.

The RSPB provided lots of encouragement and information and is active throughout the region even well away from their organised reserves. The RSPB is always working for a brighter future not just for birds and other wildlife but also for communities living and working nearby.

The National Trust always provides a friendly welcome and kept me informed of future developments thus ensuring that the book is kept up to date with developments. During my visit to Vulcan village I was made welcome by villagers who focus their activities around the local pub and its associated restaurant.

I have also been encouraged by David Bellamy who is President of the Wildlife Trusts. Many of the walks described between these covers pass through or close to areas administered by the Wildlife Trusts and they have played a major role in improving the Mersey catchment.

I must pay tribute to the editorial staff of Sigma Press who have tactfully kept me under control with regard to deadlines and grammar. I am also grateful to Marlene who typed the manuscript, joined me on the walks and assisted during the directional mapping.

Dedication

This book is for Thomas Toft Freethy who enjoyed his first serious walks during the preparation of this book. I hope that it gives him as much pleasure in the future as I have enjoyed over more years than I care to remember.

CONTENTS

SECTION 4: THE BRIDGEWATER CANAL

SECTION 5: THE IRWELL

SECTION 6: THE MERSEY VALLEY

SECTION 7: THE CHESHIRE BANK

SECTION 8: THE LIVERPOOL BANK

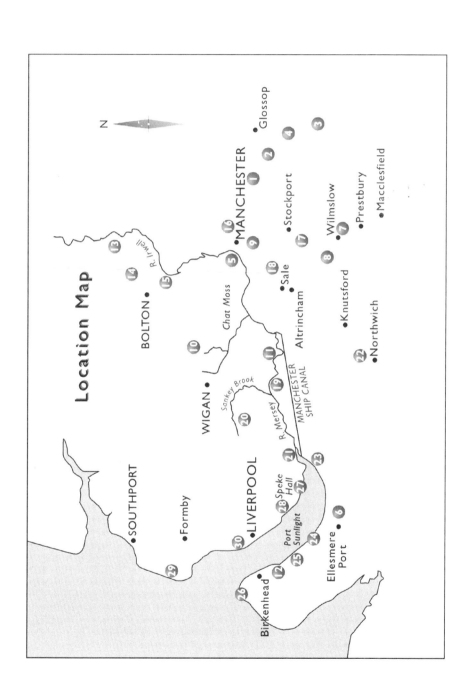

Location Map

N

SOUTHPORT

BOLTON

WIGAN

MANCHESTER

Glossop

Stockport

Wilmslow

Prestbury

Macclesfield

Sale

Altrincham

Knutsford

Northwich

Formby

LIVERPOOL

Speke Hall

Port Sunlight

Birkenhead

Ellesmere Port

R. Irwell

Chat Moss

Sankey Brook

R. Mersey

MANCHESTER SHIP CANAL

INTRODUCTION

The first reference to the River Mersey was written by the Reverend Charles Kingsley (1819-1875).

Dark and foul, dank and foul
By the smoky town with its murky cowl
Foul and dank, foul and dank
By wharf and river and slimy bank
Darker and darker the farther I go
Baser and baser the richer I grow.

The Changing River

When researching my TV documentaries, I decided to search for areas where the impact of the Industrial Revolution was either not evident or had been improved. As mentioned in the preface, I wrote a book on the Mersey and these projects meant that I have spent several years walking the banks of the Mersey and its tributaries looking for beauty spots or conducting ecological impact assessments. Even in the 1980s I found plenty of beautiful stretches and over the years many other areas have been reclaimed. My collection of postcards dating from around 1910 revealed beauty spots along the Mersey. One showed cattle grazing on the River Goyt; another was produced by Cadbury's and described the attractions of the Mersey and its catchments (see front cover).

The 1985 book largely concerned itself with the history of the river and the canals that linked into it. As a keen stroller (rather than a long distance walker) I spent many working hours and even more leisure time exploring the banks of the Mersey catchment.

I spoke to wardens, voluntary workers, officials of North West Water (now United Utilities), the Environment Agency, industrialists and anglers. I visited country parks, canal workers, naturalists and stately homes, not to mention publicans, owners of restaurants and teashops plus a host of others. Over the years I kept diaries and took thousands of photographs. I was present when new footpaths were opened – and even enjoyed cutting a few ribbons of my own.

Over the last 20 years I have noticed two things. Firstly, local ramblers are spending more time in their own catchment area and comparing it favourably with areas in the Lake District and the Dales of Derbyshire and Yorkshire. Secondly, the Mersey area and its country-

1

The River Goyt, Taxal, Whaley Bridge: a postcard from 1910, showing that not all of the
Mersey catchment was affected by industry

side are attracting more and more tourists. Apart from the history and
natural history, two other factors will prove to be a boost for tourism in
the area. These are Manchester's hosting of the Commonwealth Games
held in 2002 and the impact of Liverpool's award of the European City
of Culture in 2008.

Transport in the region has been a problem but a new road crossing
of the Mersey, and the Liverpool John Lennon Airport's facelift will
prove more of a blessing than many predict.

'Riverside Rambles along the Mersey' has excited me, as the
publisher has allowed me a lot of space (but never enough) to explore
the hundreds of miles of footpaths along the catchment. Most of the
walks are circular but where possible public transport links have meant
that linear strolls can also be enjoyed. Hotels, toilets and cafés are vital
especially as families can enjoy the Magic of the Mersey, in particular
those (like me) who are beyond the first or even the second flush of
youth.

These thirty walks are but a distillation of my favourite spots culled
from more than a quarter of a century of rambling the Mersey. The writ-
ing of this book meant that I had the incentive to return to walks, old
haunts and hostelries as well as to photograph new scenes and wildlife.

I hope that these pages inspire other strollers to follow the Mersey meanders and prove that there are so many places of interest that I have missed.

The walks have been divided into eight sections:

- The Source
- The Manchester Ship Canal
- The Bollin
- The Bridgewater Canal
- The Irwell
- The Mersey Valley
- The Cheshire Bank
- The Liverpool Bank

Whenever there are reports of ecological improvements these have to be supported by accurate environmental assessments. Only in comparatively recent times have biodiversity studies become important. Some, but thankfully not all, academics have ignored the valuable data from so-called amateur naturalists. There is no substitute for experience and in this brief ecological survey given here, I have gathered information from many naturalists – including seven who are well over seventy and have been studying the Mersey and its wildlife for many years.

A brief ecological history of the Mersey

It is hard to imagine these days that from the 12th century the lucrative fishing rights were jealously guarded. The rights on the Cheshire side were shared between the Constable of Chester and the Augustinian Priory of Norton (see walk 12).

Why were these fishing rights so jealously guarded? Salmon were present in great abundance, as were mullet, sand eels, sturgeon and the 'largest cockles in England'.

From the 14th century, there was some conflict between the fishermen and the trading ships. The fishermen wanted to keep their fish alive until their customers arrived and they therefore set up structures called puts. These were huge wicker baskets that functioned just like an angler's keep net. They were, however, situated close to the centre of the river and the boatmen regarded them as a hazard to navigation.

In 1792 the fishery at Warrington was worth £400 per annum – a huge enterprise at this time. The catch included sturgeon, salmon (some more than 40 pounds in weight) and sparling, which is an old name for the smelt. In 1824 one Warrington fishmonger made enough from the species to build a row of houses, which he called Sparling Row.

The smelt (*Osmerus eperlanus*) is a small, silvery almost translucent fish related to the whitebait group. They are excellent to eat and occur in estuaries but also migrate into 'fresh' water to breed. Until the days of the Industrial Revolution, they occurred in huge numbers. From the 1870s, the effect of pollutants began to be felt and by the end of the Second World War, commercial fishing on the Mersey had ceased.

Although scientific studies of fish populations were not carried out until the late 1990s it is obvious that by the 1960s fish were absent from most of the Mersey catchment. As fish are a vital component in the food chain this meant that fish-eating birds such as the heron and the kingfisher were missing from the catchment. Otters, which were once resident throughout the catchment, disappeared once there was nothing for them to eat. Let us hope that the Otter's Pool on the Liverpool bank of the Mersey, Otterspool Bridge on the Goyt and the woodlands around Reddish Vale on the Tame will eventually support this lovely mammal once more (see walks 1, 4 and 20).

Improvements were dramatic during the 1990s. The decline of many industries has led to an increase in water quality, but other factors also have to be acknowledged. United Utilities (01925 233988), the water company covering the North West of England, has played a vital role by constructing water treatment and sewage works, whilst the Environment Agency has played an equally vital role in pushing through environmental legislation.

United Utilities is very conscious of the wildlife in and around their water collecting areas but they also welcome walkers. Many reservoirs have circular walks around them, and if these are followed the 30 walks described in this book could easily be doubled!

The Mersey Basin Campaign (0161 242 8200), set up in 1985 and set to run until at least 2010, has publicised the success of the clean-up operation. It continues to function with great efficiency.

This success has not produced complacency but improvements have continued apace. One of the most polluted areas in the catchment was around Warrington especially at Woolston Weir. In the early 1980s when I visited the area the smell was apparent from a good distance away whilst detergent generated foam bubbled over the weir. When the

Will the otter return to parts of the Mersey? There are optimistic signs.

wind blew, foam was carried over long distance. This was a place to avoid.

In 2002 the Environment Agency set up a humane fish trap at Woolston Weir and to say that the results were exciting would be an understatement. During the autumn run of October and November, 26 salmon were caught and released. Other important species recorded were sea trout, brown trout, dace and lamprey.

All these species are important as indicators of improving water quality but there can be no doubt that the headlines are grabbed by the return of the Atlantic salmon.

Three other organisations have also been instrumental in promoting ecological improvements of the region. These are the Royal Society for the Protection of Birds (RSPB, tel: 01484 861148) and the two Community Forests. The Red Rose Forest operates around Manchester whilst the Mersey Forest concerns itself with improvements close to Liverpool and the Wirral. The local Wildlife Trusts are also playing a major role in conservation. The RSPB does not just concern itself with bird reserves but takes an interest in the welfare of birds and does excellent work in the Mersey catchment. The Society has widened its brief to involve the welfare of all flora and fauna.

The two Community Forests, like the Mersey Basin Campaign, are government funded and worth every penny. The Forests have excellent tree planting programmes and provide lots of valuable information on ecology. The Red Rose Forest: 0161 872 1660. The Mersey Forest: 01925 859 604.

The Wildlife Trusts are also playing a vital role and walkers who join these organisations will soon find their list of locations increased. Those who enjoy company whilst walking will also find a welcome. The Lancashire Wildlife Trust: 01772 324129. The Cheshire Wildlife Trust: 01270 610180.

These and other organisations are keen to build up their ecological database and welcome records of fauna and flora. The more comprehensive these lists are the easier it is to conserve some of the more vulnerable species found in the Mersey catchment. This applies to species such as kingfisher, stonechat, common sandpiper and even once numerous species such as song thrush and house sparrow, which have declined during the 1990s.

It is also important to record mammals with the otter being most important but badger, fox and brown hare should also be recorded especially when in an urban setting. This also applies to bats.

Plants are also important and some areas have turned up real surprises. The paint company H. Marcel Guest, for example, has landscaped an old chemical works on the banks of the River Irk close to the centre of Manchester and set up a private nature reserve; tel: 0161 2057631. Here the alkaline chemical has encouraged the growth of orchids and such plants as centaury, which are normally associated with sand dunes. It is a sign of the times that such companies should take an interest in the environment and spend money on it without being compelled to do it. The benefit is that the workforce has a wonderful area in which to sit whilst enjoying their lunch in the summertime (see also walk 15).

Such ecological treasures can be found during each and every one of the 30 walks covered in this book and I am now in the happy position of being able to write positively about the history and natural history of the Mersey catchment.

SECTION 1: THE SOURCE

Anyone who wishes to study the catchment of the Mersey must begin high on the hills towards Old Yorkshire and Derbyshire. There is also a fair slice of Cheshire to be found along the trio of major tributaries.

The Mersey, as a name, begins at Stockport and was the natural boundary between the counties of Cheshire, Lancashire and Yorkshire. The name itself simply means 'boundary river'. This would seem to suggest that a huge torrent of water flushes out under the modern conurbation of Stockport. Actually the three tributaries meet close by and those who want riverside rambles in search of the Mersey must stroll along each.

It is to the Normans that we owe the origins of the present county system. Before their arrival, most of the Mersey catchment was in Mercia, but at times the Kings of Northumbria were not averse to raiding into the Tame, Etherow and Goyt valleys. In early Christian times, the area was ruled from Lichfield and the bishop was Chad who ruled from AD669 until AD672 when he died of plague (see walk 4).

The Tame

From its source on Saddleworth Moor, the Tame meanders through Mossley, Stalybridge, Dukinfield, Ashton-under-Lyne and then on to Hyde and its meeting with the Goyt and Etherow complex near Stockport. Its name is of Celtic origin and means 'dark river'. This does not mean that the Celts found it polluted but indicated that, from its source, the river was stained with the peat so typical of our northern moorlands. Along the 20-mile meander to the Mersey confluence there are clear and twinkling sections whilst other stretches have not recovered from the pollution of the Industrial Revolution.

There is pleasant walking country around the Tame including the Reddish Vale Trail and the Roaches Trail, which are organised by the Tame Valley Warden Service. In the first of the riverside rambles in this book, we explore Reddish Vale but there are upland and middle reach reaches, which provide wonderful walks.

The Etherow

This river was said to rise at the junction of the old counties of Cheshire,

Yorkshire and Lancashire. Long before this, the Etherow flowed close to an ancient green road and the Romans built a fort to protect the routes leading towards Chester. Later still, road, canal and rail links followed the route, as industry demanded easier import and export infrastructures.

These industries demanded more and more water and the present-day upper catchment of the Etherow runs into and out of a series of impressive reservoirs. The Longdendale system has trails around each reservoir and United Utilities have provided free guides. Most of the once-prosperous mills have long gone but the Etherow Country Park is based around Compstall Mill.

The Goyt

The source of the Goyt is close to the Cat and Fiddle Inn in Derbyshire, where a boggy area smells of hydrogen sulphide and oozes stinking water over the walkers' boots. The Goyt Valley has been flooded, as the demand for water especially around Manchester grew more insistent. The Errwood reservoir, built as late as the 1960s, supplemented the flow of the earlier and much larger Fernilee reservoir. The loss of this submerged area to pure historians has been somewhat compensated by the gain to natural historians, as both waters have become the haunt of wildfowl. The surrounding plantations and uplands are the breeding grounds of rare birds of prey such as hen harrier. In these areas the RSPB and United Utilities make a perfect conservation team.

United Utilities, which owns much of the upper catchment, has also worked hard to protect wildlife and to make walkers welcome. Many free publications are available and point out circular walks around the reservoirs. Because of this, the walking routes are easy and there is lots to enjoy. One of the most fascinating areas in the Goyt Valley is known as the Roman Lakes. But how Roman are they? Those who follow Walk 3 will discover much of interest.

Once the Goyt has swallowed the Etherow, it continues towards Marple and passes beneath the arches of the aqueduct carrying the Peak Forest Canal. To the east of Stockport is Chadkirk Country Park – some 59 acres (24 hectares) of glorious walking – but there is also a working farm and an old chapel now functioning as an Information Centre (see walk 4). Close by, the Goyt joins the Tame and the name of the dual flow is changed to the Mersey.

Walk 1: Reddish Vale and The Tame

Directions: From the M60 exit at Junction 24. Follow the A57 towards Manchester. Continue to Reddish South Railway Station. Soon after crossing the railway bridge approach traffic lights. Turn left onto Reddish Vale Road. Carry straight on past a secondary school on the left. Continue straight ahead down a cul-de-sac. Pass Reddish Vale Small Animal Farm and Tea Room on the right and a row of cottages on the left. Continue ahead to Reddish Vale Country Park and Nature Reserve Car Park (free). There is a Visitor Centre, tel: 0161 477 5637.

Public Transport: Reddish South Railway Station within easy walking distance.Buses from Stockport (Nos.7, 203 and 319). For local bus and train information ring 0161 228 7811.

Map Reference: OS Explorer 277 Grid Reference 910 935

Distance: 6 miles

Time: 2½ hours

The name 'Reddish' dates from Robert de Reddish who settled in the area in 1181. The word is Old English and translates as 'Reedy Ditch' – still true of some places along this walk today. Riverside meanders came to a halt in the 1790s when a calico printing works was built. 'Calico' is undyed cotton fabric and there was a town in India of this name which exported the fabric to England. As raw cotton was imported from the New World from the 18th century onwards, the Indian city lost its trade but the word has remained. The Reddish works dyed calico and there must have been times when the Tame was multicoloured. The peak period of the Reddish works was between 1860 and 1930 although production did not cease for a further forty years.

Much industrial archaeology can be enjoyed during this walk but farming never completely disappeared. This is why the walk should be combined with a visit to the Reddish Vale Farm. A variety of animals can be seen, to the delight of children, whilst adults will enjoy the museum which focuses on a comparison between ancient and modern farming methods.

There is a tea room and this and the farm have opening times that vary according to the season. Farm and Museum: 0161 4801645. Tea shop: 0161 480 0084.

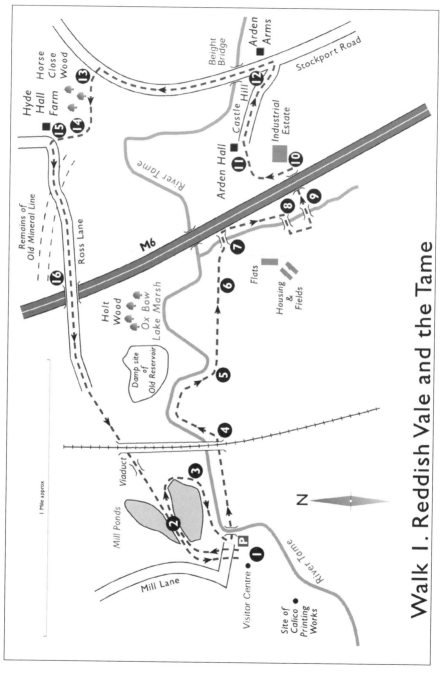

Walk I. Reddish Vale and the Tame

The print works pond and the viaduct at Reddish Vale

The Route

1. The Visitors' Centre has an exhibition area, which sets the whole area in context. From the centre, pass through the car park to the mill ponds. Obviously, these were excavated to provide essential water for the print works. In medieval times there was a watermill which ground cereals and which was powered by the River Tame. This was demolished when the ponds were constructed.

These are now the haunts of birds – especially wildfowl – but there are areas of fringing vegetation providing ideal habitat for reed buntings. This species has become less common in recent years because of loss of habitat. Old industrial sites such as Reddish have a vital role to play in redressing the balance.

2. Follow one of two of the obvious circular trails around the ponds. Both of these sweep right and visible to the left is the magnificent railway viaduct. This was built in 1875 by the Sheffield and Midland Railway Company and is still in regular use today.

3. Continue towards the River Tame and then turn right. Keep the river on the left and a pond to the right. Approach the car park but bear sharp left before this and cross a bridge over the river. The Tame is now on the left. Continue along the obvious path to the viaduct immediately ahead.

4. Cross under the viaduct and ignore the more obvious track straight ahead. Turn left alongside the viaduct on the left and approach the river. The Tame hereabouts looks idyllic and can have changed little over the centuries. Away in the distance, however, is a stark reminder of 21st-century living – the M60 motorway always seems to be busy.

5. Sweep right and follow the path which gradually veers away from the river. Beyond the opposite bank is Holt Wood. As the otters breeding area is called a Holt we must assume that until the Industrial Revolution otters were common all along the Mersey catchment. We must hope that in time these lovely creatures will return, as has been the case with badgers. At this point and others along this route there is a complex network of footpaths. If in any doubt always take the path to the left.

6. Pass through an area of woodland full of flowers in spring and fungi in autumn. Grey squirrels are very common here. **Caution:** this area can be very wet and slippery and appropriate footwear should be worn. Cross some small footbridges along the straight path.

7. Approach a substantial footbridge. Continue over this and pass through the woodland. Through the trees to the right the urban aspect can be seen with blocks of high-rise flats evident. This view is much clearer in the winter when the trees are leafless. Away to the left (but out of sight) the sound of the M60 traffic starts to increase.

8. Approach an even more substantial bridge crossing a steep ravine in which flows a tributary stream. Cross this, turn left, and go along a footpath skirting the wooded ravine. To the right there are fields and beyond these a substantial housing complex and flats.

9. Keep to the left until a footbridge is reached. Turn left and first cross this bridge and immediately after is another footbridge this time crossing over the busy M60. Within a short distance of the motorway, wildlife continues to thrive and in the spring bird song can almost drown the sound of traffic.

Arden Hall – once an important manor house, now a farm

A Choice

There is plenty to see by continuing this walk but it has to be admitted that this involves a more urban setting and there is some walking along a busy road. Any student of the Mersey and its catchments, however, has to accept and admire the way that these watercourses have adapted to changes. Those who decide not to retrace their steps will need courage initially.

10. At the end of the footbridge turn left along a very narrow footpath usually blighted by litter. A stout fence to the right protects a large commercial complex, which to the walker has only one bright spot. On the roadside is a caravan serving the usual snacks adored by workers – especially lorry drivers.

Follow this track with the M60 away in a dip to the left and then bear sharp right. To the left are (usually) grazing cattle, which seem to have been part of the landscape for centuries. Ahead and to the left is Arden Hall. Follow an overgrown path, which can be difficult to negotiate in summer.

11. Pass through metal gates and then left to the substantial farmhouse known as Arden Hall. In 1350 this place was known as Harden and is Saxon in origin. Some think that this translates as a "place inhabited by hares".

Continue along Battle Lane, which could have had a Civil War link because it is said that Cromwell lodged at the hall for a night.

12. Continue along Battle Lane with Castle Hill to the left. Although all traces have now gone, there was a small fortification on this spot but it may well have been Saxon and made of wood. On the left is a cottage, which was in Victorian times an inn, which served tea to walkers. They could also buy hot water and brew their own.

Approach the busy Stockport Road. Turn left and see the Arden Arms pub on the right. Cross the substantial Beight Bridge over the River Tame and then a sewage works to the left.

13. Keep a look out for a sign indicating Hyde Hall Farm. Turn left.

14. Pass Horse Close Wood to the right and keep a sharp look out to the left. Here is all that is left of the ill-fated Beight Bank Canal. This began with a flourish in the 1790s and was a private venture, intended to link with the Ashton Canal. It was never completed as it ran out of cash.

15. Approach Hyde Hall farm. Its architecture is a fascinating blend of 15th- and 16th-century styles. It has been a farm since the early 19th century but it is easy both to appreciate its pedigree and to understand why it is a listed building.

Turn left along Ross Lave Lane. Look out for a long-disused mineral railway line, which once led to coal mines and which crosses this route.

16. Cross the M60 motorway and continue along Ross Lane. Pass under the viaduct and over a footbridge. Return to the Visitors' Centre via the pond area. If the weather is good, here is an ideal place for a picnic but you will have to share your food with the wildfowl.

Walk 2: Etherow Country Park at Compstall

Directions: The Country Park is surrounded by a veritable spider's web of major and minor roads. Be patient, however, and follow the A6 towards Marple and look for the B6104 road. The Country Park is 1½ miles to the north-east of Marple. *At Marple Bridge, be sure to take a left turn immediately after crossing the bridge.* There is a large Pay-and-display car park (modest charges). Here too are an Information Centre, café and toilet facilities; tel: 0161 427 6937

Public Transport: The Country Park is within walking distance of Marple Railway station and a local bus service links Compstall to Marple.

Map Reference: OS Explorer 277 Grid Reference 975 915

Distance: 5 miles when all suggested diversions are taken

Time: Allow 3 hours

The atmospheric village of Compstall owes its existence to the fiscal ambitions of the Andrews family. In the early 19th century they enlarged a hamlet, consisting of only a few cottages, into an industrial but still attractive village. Before 1820, the brothers George and Thomas set up the Andrews Company initially involved in the dyeing and printing of cotton. Realising the potential they expanded into spinning and weaving. Their ambition was helped by the construction of a new turnpike road, which sliced through the mills and reduced transport costs. By 1840 their mill was, to say the least, impressive and was surrounded by some 200 purpose-built mill workers' houses.

Why did the Andrews brothers choose to locate at Compstall? One does not have to look very far to appreciate the reason – the fast flowing River Etherow. Although the river was there, the company still had a great deal of engineering work to do. They built a huge weir, extensive millponds, a millrace and two mighty water wheels. Some of these structures are still evident today. Later on, as steam replaced waterpower, coal was essential and at nearby Ernocroft there were large deposits of this mineral.

The Andrews clan comprised hard workers and imaginative engineers but their fortunes were also assisted by "geological luck". At

15

Ernocroft there were, in addition to coal seams, large deposits of fire clay, which was ideal for the manufacture of bricks and tiles. All these deposits show that the Etherow flows through a steep gorge that was ground out by melt water as the last Ice Age loosened its grip around 10,000 years ago.

So successful was the Compstall Mill complex that it only ceased to function in 1966. An enterprising local authority realised that here was an ideal opportunity to develop a country park. This now consists of two separate elements. Firstly, the cotton mill with its associated lodges, reservoirs and weirs has proved an ideal habitat for waterfowl such as mallard, tufted duck, pochard, Canada geese and mute swans. Kingfishers often sparkle in the sunshine whilst coot and moorhen also find suitable breeding habitat. By 1971 the Park had taken shape and since this time the pollution load on the river has been reduced to almost nil. The Etherow is now even more attractive to wildlife as it was in the Middle Ages.

The second element of the Country Park, which covers 162 acres (65.5 hectares), is known as Keg Woodlands. Keg House was initially a hunting lodge but all shooting is now outlawed there. The tree species include Scots pine, wych elm, hazel, oak, ash and sycamore.

The Country Park is the Etherow's last glorious stand. Just beyond this point, it flows into Brabyns Park, where it joins the Goyt. The name Etherow disappears and the Goyt flows on into Marple Dale. The union of the two rivers is called, appropriately, Waters Meeting.

The Route

1. Begin at the car park and do a spot of bird watching by the side of the reservoir using one of the numerous seats. From the reservoir approach the Visitor Centre and café. Turn right and follow the obvious path.

2. On the left is the Etherow Garden Centre. This is open every day (0161 427 1440). Continue along the track. There are extensive areas of grass with plenty of seats overlooking pretty cottages, most kept in splendid state of repair.

3. Continue on and look for a farm gate on the left and a stretch of water (locally called the canal) on the right. Carry straight on with a row of modern housing on the left.

4. Emerge from the track onto a metalled road for a short distance. Look for a sign indicating Hirst Cottages and White Bottom Farm.

Walk 2. Etherow Country Park

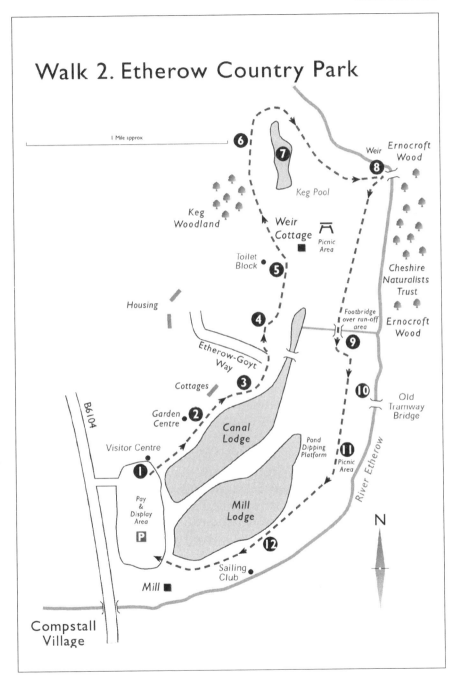

I Mile approx

⑥

⑦

Weir   Ernocroft
Wood

Keg Pool

⑧

Keg
Woodland

Weir
Cottage   Picnic
Area

Toilet
Block   ⑤

Cheshire
Naturalists
Trust

Housing

④

Footbridge
over run-off
area   Ernocroft
Wood

⑨

Etherow-Goyt
Way

Cottages

③

⑩   Old
Tramway
Bridge

B6104

Garden
Centre   ②

Canal
Lodge

Pond
Dipping
Platform   ⑪

Picnic
Area

River Etherow

Visitor Centre

①

Pay
&
Display
Area

Mill
Lodge

N

P

⑫

Mill ■

Sailing
Club

Compstall
Village

Keep right and follow a track marked the "Etherow-Goyt Way". Continue straight ahead and ignore all footbridges to the right over the River Goyt.

5. Continue to Hirst Cottages but look to the right in a dip. Here are the skeletal remains of the horse-drawn coal barges, which date from around 1820. They once loaded coal from the drift mines in Ernocroft Wood. Several barges were linked together – the horse provided the power and the whole train was steered by a boatman's tiller operated from the last barge on the line.

Look up to the left where there are good toilets, whilst to the right there is a picnic site. Follow the path around the rear of Hirst Cottage, into Keg Wood.

6. On no account should Keg Wood be rushed, as local folk often deliver food for birds especially in winter and the site is not only the haunt of common species but also the occasional rarity such as woodcock and buzzard.

7. Keg Pool also provides lots of ornithological interest but the surroundings are equally attractive in the summer. Here are dragonflies, damselflies, toads, frogs, newts and a variety of colourful flowers. Continue onwards until the bridge over the Etherow and the weir are reached.

8. The Etherow weir would seem at first glance to be an engineering feat built for the Andrews family. This is true but prior to this the Etherow tumbled down into its valley via a cascade of natural waterfalls. The acceleration caused by the weir bubbles oxygen into the water. This oxygen increases the number of invertebrates such as mayfly and stonefly. These provide food for trout and other fish as well as birds such as resident dipper and grey wagtails plus summer visiting common sandpiper. Herons, always on the look out for food, are seen throughout the year.

9. Close to the bridge look out for the Woodland Nature Reserve running through Ernocroft Woods. Visitors should ask for a permit to visit which can be obtained from the Visitors' Centre. The reserve is run by the Cheshire Wildlife Trust (01270 610180). A network of footpaths runs around the reserve. Return to the bridge, cross it and look left.

10. Turn left and follow the path through the picnic site. Cross over a long wooden footbridge. There is a canal on the right whilst the River Etherow is below to the left. Excess water is run off at this point from the canal into the river.

Continue ahead and look out for a sign pointing to the Old Tramway Bridge. The bridge has long gone but a look across the river reveals the stone supports of the span. This allowed coal from Ernocroft mine to be transported over the Etherow to the canal barges waiting on the opposite bank.

11. Continue onwards keeping the canal on the right and the Etherow on the left.

Canada Geese at Etherow Country Park

There are several large bird tables on the left and soon a small picnic site is reached. At the picnic site the route back to the Visitors' Centre diverges. Take the left fork. To the right is a notice indicating the aquatic wildlife to be seen in the area. There is also a platform used by school parties to pond dip.

Approach the large reservoir to the right. To the left are numerous seats donated in memory of people who had enjoyed their strolls around the Etherow Country Park. The reservoir is a fine example of how to develop a multi-purpose amenity. Using the route are dog walkers, joggers, anglers, naturalists, wheelchair users and sometimes there are boats with colourful sails sweeping across the water.

12. On the left pass the Etherow Country Park Sailing Club. Bear right and return to the car park.

Walk 3: Along the Goyt – The Roman Lakes

Directions: Marple is around 4 miles to the west of Stockport and reached via the M60 motorway. Exit at Junction 25 and follow the signs for Bredbury and Marple Bridge (not Marple). Take care at Marple Bridge – cross the bridge and bear left. Almost immediately, turn left along Arkwright Road. Keep a sharp look out for a small sign to the left indicating Roman Lakes. Follow the rough track called Lakes Road to the car park. Most of the facilities at Roman Lakes are free and this also applies to the car park.

Public Transport: Marple has two railway stations, which are at Rose Hill and Marple itself. Rosehill is the closer to the Roman Lakes and is about one mile away. There are radio-linked taxis well used to delivering passengers to and from the lakes. 1919 Taxis are on 0161 494 1919 and Metro Taxis on 0161 480 8000.

Facilities: The centre is open every day except Christmas Day. From Monday to Friday the times are 08.00 to dusk and at weekends from 07.30 to dusk. Available free at the café are leaflets on the history and natural history of the area. Visitors pay a fee for angling, mountain bikes can be hired and there is also a boules court (see walk 17). Tel/Fax: 0161 427 2039 Web site: www.romanlakes.co.uk. Fishing courses (especially for pike) are run during the winter.

Map Reference: OS Explorer OL1 Grid Reference 973 882

Distance: 4½ miles

Time: 2½ hours

It is often said that the name 'Roman Lakes' was invented by the Victorians to attract visitors. Some feel, however, there may be facts to suggest a Roman influence. The hills above the Lakes were certainly used as an ancient highway. At this time, the valley of the Goyt was a malaria-ridden swamp and suitable crossing points over the river were few and far between.

There was an ancient ford at the place occupied by a packhorse span now known as the Roman Bridge. The local settlement of Mellor is significant as it derives from the ancient Celtic (Welsh) word Moelfre

meaning a 'bare hill' i.e.
barren of trees and therefore
easier walking. It is interesting that at another Mellor
close to the River Ribble
near Blackburn there was a
Roman signal station. It may
well be that there was a similar structure high above the
Goyt.

After the Romans came
first the Anglo Saxons and
then the Normans. The
kings and nobles of the
Normans fiercely defended
their   hunting   forests
throughout England. One of
these (Macclesfield) forests
stretched between the then
pristine   rivers   of   the
Etherow and the Goyt.

No doubt there were peri-
ods of peace in Norman
England and large areas

The old packhorse bridge

came under the control of monasteries. Newburgh Abbey in Yorkshire
owned much land around the Goyt.

Later came the Industrial Revolution and King Cotton proved to be
an increasingly thirsty monarch. The substantial Bottoms Mill built by
Samuel Oldknow (1756-1828) on the banks of the Goyt soon involved
the construction of huge water wheels and later a series of ponds to
provide steam power. These form the basis of the present Roman Lakes
Leisure Parks.

The Route

1. From the Roman Lakes car park, walk to the road and turn left with
   the Goyt on the right towards the viaduct. Look out for a weir. This
   is best seen in winter when the leaves are off the trees. At this time
   look out for heron and goosander on the river.

2. Pass under the railway viaduct. This opened in 1865 on the line

linking Manchester and Sheffield. It is still in use today and a fine example of Victorian engineering. In the winter of 2003-2004 the viaduct was repaired without the busy line having to be closed. Prior to the work commencing a detailed ecological assessment was carried out especially relating to potential bat roosts.

3. Just beyond the viaduct on the left of the now unmade road is Floodgates Cottage. The present house, which dates to 1804, was originally two cottages. The sluice operator occupied one and, as the name of the building indicates, the water levels of the Goyt were adjusted to feed the lakes. The second cottage was occupied by the toll keeper, who collected money from those using the narrow road, now reduced in importance. There are hinges on the wall that once supported the gates of the tollhouse.

4. Follow the narrow track and look out for a right turn leading down to the Packhorse Bridge. Cross the bridge and take care to avoid slipping on the moss-covered steps. Note the arrangement of the stones on the bridge floor that were designed to prevent horses slipping.

The bridge is thought to have been built around 1700 with the iron railings over the span added about a century later. Signs of the ancient ford possibly even pre-Roman can be detected at times of low rainfall.

From the bridge follow the woodland path uphill between two houses. Continue straight ahead and cross Strines Road. Climb a hill and ascend steps.

5. These steps lead onto the towpath of the Peak Forest Canal. This was built in two halves with a bit of a problem between. One section was opened for business in 1796 but the lower canal was not finally completed until 1800.

The Upper (Buxworth or Bugsworth) level and the Lower (Marple to Ashton) level giving a total of 14 miles had a gap in the middle due to lack of finance. Samuel Oldknow was ambitious with regard to cotton and canals but was not the best businessman. He was helped out by the Arkwrights, who eventually absorbed his family undertakings. By 1805 (Trafalgar year) the horse-drawn tramway constructed to link the gap was replaced by a series of locks.

Walk 3. Roman Lakes and River Goyt

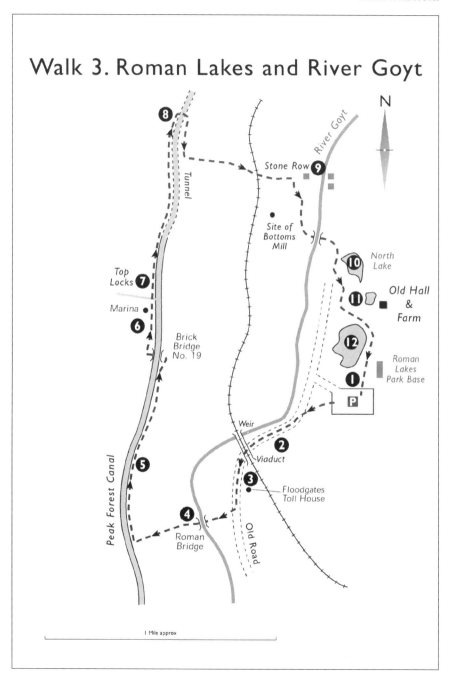

N

River Goyt

Stone Row 9

Tunnel

Site of
Bottoms
Mill

North
Lake

10

Top
Locks 7

11

Old Hall
&
Farm

Marina

6

Brick
Bridge
No. 19

12

Roman
Lakes
Park Base

1

P

2

Weir

Viaduct

3

Floodgates
Toll House

Peak Forest Canal

5

4

Roman
Bridge

Old Road

1 Mile approx

23

6. Follow the towpath bearing right under a bridge and continue to bridge number 19 also known as the 'brick bridge'. Here the towpath changes sides. Turn right and continue to a fascinating area. This is Marple Marina and very popular with boaters.

7. Follow the locks and pass through a tunnel over a main road, which was substantial enough to allow both barges and horses to pass through.

    After the tunnel follow the towpath to another set of locks and turn right across the canal and then right again along the opposite towpath.

8. Pass a converted canal warehouse on the left and then read the street names, which bring back memories of cotton. Look for Oldknow Road. Turn left and then cross Arkwright Road. Faywood Drive leads to Lakes Road.

9. Turn right and look to the left to find Stone Row. Although Bottoms Mill was destroyed by fire in 1892, its six storeys made up what was then the world's largest cotton spinning mill. Oldknow also built Stone Row cottages for his workers and here he also had a shop which his workers had to patronise. In comparison with other less scrupulous employers Oldknow was fair but he was still able to charge above the odds for provisions. This "Tommy Shop" was traditional throughout Lancashire and the practice was only stopped when the Rochdale Pioneers set up their own workers' shop on Toad Lane. This evolved into the modern Cooperative Wholesale Society. All who shopped were given an annual dividend and many workers were reliant on their 'divi' being paid at certain times.

    Away to the right is the old site of Bottom Mill. All that now remains are a few of the foundations close to the River Goyt and in summer almost concealed by a tangle of vegetation.

10. Cross Bottoms Bridge and turn right. Pass North Lake on the left. This is the smaller of the Roman Lakes. Continue along the obvious path and look left.

11. Old Hall and Farm provide another chapter in the history of Samuel Oldknow's contribution to the annals of textiles. Old Hall was there before the mill was constructed. The adjacent farm was built by Oldknow to provide accommodation to house his 'appren-

tices', which was a polite word for child labourers. These were mainly girls brought from the streets and orphanages around Clerkenwell in London.

Oldknow followed the same system for finding labour as the Gregs at Styal on the Bollin (see walk 7). Before we condemn the Gregs and the Oldknows, we should not forget that other employers, and even parents, treated children much worse than these textile families.

12. Continue onwards to the path around the Main Lake. This is now an important fishery especially for carp and pike but there are other species also well worth fishing for. These include roach, bream and tench. The water level varies between 2 and 6 feet (0.7 and 2 metres). Carp, which can reach 30 pounds (14kgs), were introduced in the 1950s and have developed as a major fishery. The pike have been brought in as eggs on the feet of wildfowl and specimens have been caught in excess of 20 pounds (9kg).

The Roman Lakes area is of major importance for birdwatching and species lists can be obtained from the café. The water levels are now maintained by natural drainage from tributary streams leading down towards the Goyt.

Rowing boats are still for hire as they have been for over a century. Near the boathouse is an old turnstile which operated when the entry fee of one old penny was inserted. These days, entry is free. Continue from the lakes and return to the car park.

Walk 4: Chadkirk and Marple

Directions: Take the M60 and turn off at Junction 25. Follow the A560 towards Bredbury and then the A627 towards Marple. Look out for a sign to Chadkirk just beyond Otterspool Bridge over the River Goyt. There is a car park for Chadkirk Country Estate.

Public Transport: The railway station at Rosehill is actually on the circular walk and this could therefore be used as a base rather than Chadkirk car park.

Map Reference: OS Explorer OL1 Grid Reference 944 895

Distance: 5 miles

Time: 2½ hours

It is difficult to understand why some historians have suggested that there is no evidence to support the belief that St Chad operated in this area. Who was St Chad? He was a missionary who was the Bishop of Lichfield from AD 669 to AD 672 when he died of the plague.

There is no doubt that he was active in the North West of England and founded a major church at Poulton-le-Fylde. Why is this area called Chadkirk if St Chad was not involved? Medieval records suggest that 'Chadchappel' was a monkish cell. Nearby is a well and these places were important to pilgrims who thought that springs had healing powers. Most of these pre-dated Christian times and in many areas of Derbyshire 'well dressing' is a feature dating back to Celtic times.

A deed of 1347 cites a conveyance of land from one William de Halton to a chaplain named as William de Chadkirk. There must therefore have been a religious settlement prior to this. The present chapel, even sceptical historians admit, "was built to a Saxon pattern". This suggests that there was probably a wooden structure here that was later copied in stone.

In 1560, during the reign of Henry VIII, the Chantry's income was valued at four pounds one shilling and sixpence. During the Tudor-Stuart period, Chadkirk was a hotbed of the Protestant faith and this continued until 1706 when a new chapel was built at nearby Hatherlow.

Chadkirk appears to have been neglected until 1746 when there was a substantial rebuild, followed by additions and restorations in 1761,

1860 and 1876. The chapel is centred upon a working farm of 59 acres (24 hectares) and the complex was purchased by the go-ahead Bredbury and Romily Urban District Council. This was taken over by the Metropolitan Borough of Stockport in 1979 and developed as a Country Estate in the Goyt Valley.

Visitors should not enter the farm buildings without permission but there are plenty of notice boards explaining the complex. Here is a real farm run at a profit rather than a lifeless museum. Details can be obtained by ringing 0161 427 6937

Chadkirk chapel and garden

The Route

1. From the car park turn left onto the narrow winding road. Look out for a gate to the right. Pass through the gate and cross a field to a second gate. Go through this.

2. To the right is an extensive picnic area and the route into Kirkwood. This is described as 'ancient' woodland and this means that it was in existence prior to 1600. Such woodlands are of vital importance as the Mersey catchment has lost most of these especially during the Industrial Revolution.

3. Follow the obvious footpath with Kirkwood on the right and turn left into Chadkirk chapel grounds with the farm behind it.

   Inside the chapel, a slight adaptation has provided an exhibition area with audiovisual material. The chapel is open on Saturday and Sunday afternoons and the little coffee shop does good business.

The area surrounding the chapel consists of a herb garden with the plants labelled and classified into species associated with herbal and culinary subjects. Here are specimens of digitalis (foxglove), chamomile, lovage, bistort and monkshood.

Set among the plants are items of old farm machinery especially ploughs but also in evidence are some sculptures such as deer, which have been woven from twigs.

4. From the chapel turn right and pass the farm also on the right. Continue to ascend and reach St-Chad's Well on the left. As at the chapel the history of the well is described in the form of an illustrated display board. The well is in a good state of repair and it would be good to follow the Derbyshire tradition by organising a well dressing. Continue to ascend the path and towards the summit look out for a set of steps.

5. Ascend these steps and turn right along the towpath of the Peak Forest Canal. This was built between 1794 and 1801 largely at the instigation of Samuel Oldknow (see walk 3). The incentive was to provide an essential transport link for cotton and quarry stone. The transport from quarry to canal was organised by Thomas Pickford's company, which began to operate in the 1640s. By the 1680s, their carts were carrying stone as far as London and this was used to pave the streets. The Company was in search of a use for their empty wagons during the return journey. This is how the removal company, which is still important today, originated. Pickfords were not slow to adapt to canal and rail, and now to the motorway system.

6. Continue along the towpath and approach Hyde Bank Tunnel. There is no towpath inside the tunnel and, until replaced by steam and then diesel, the barges were propelled by human power. These specialist men were known as 'leggers' and they moved heavy loads by pushing their feet against the sides of tunnels. Here we have the origin of the term "to leg it".

The horses had a chance to drink at the horse trough and were then led over the present footpath. Follow the path over the tunnel, pass a farm and then bear right back down to the towpath.

7. Cross the Marple Aqueduct, built by the engineer Benjamin Outram and opened in 1800. The aqueduct soars more than 100

Walk 4. Chadkirk and Marple

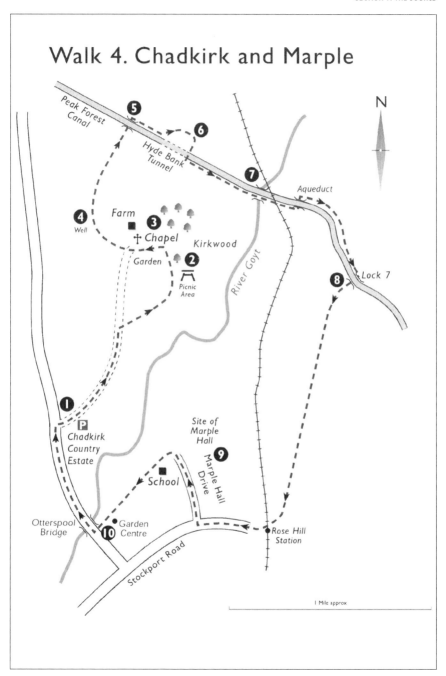

feet over the River Goyt. Nearby is the much larger railway viaduct, which also crosses the Goyt. During the winter of 1962-63 the frost was so prolonged and so severe that the aqueduct and nearby locks were damaged and there was a threat to abandon the canal. Thankfully the Peak Forest Canal Society took a hand and this area is now an attractive location.

8. Continue along the towpath to Lock 7. Cross the bridge close to the bottom gates and follow the obvious route until the junction with Winnington Road. Cross this and follow Grosvenor Road. When Manor Road is reached look for a footpath known as Seven Stiles.

Follow the boundary of Marple Cricket Club and, at the end of Bowden Lane, turn right over a railway bridge. Then turn left onto Dale Road and then Rosehill Station and onto Stockport Road.

9. Look for a zebra crossing and cross this before turning right onto Marple Hall Drive. The ruins of Marple Hall should be looked at closely because here is a major slice of Mersey history.

Marple Hall was the birthplace of the infamous John Bradshaw. We think of graffiti and vandalism as a modern phenomenon but John may well have been one of the worst. He was baptised at Stockport on 18th December 1602. Whilst at school at Macclesfield John Bradshaw carved an inscription on the church wall:

My brother Henry must heir the land
My brother Frank must be at his command
Whilst I, poor Jack will do that
That all the world must wonder at

John Bradshaw began his working life as clerk to a Congleton lawyer, but by 1627 he was called to the bar at Gray's Inn in London. His skills were such that by 1637 he returned to Congleton rich enough to become mayor. He never made any secret of the fact that he preferred a republic to a monarchy. At the conclusion of the Civil War he became the first and only commoner to judge and condemn to death his reigning monarch. Bradshaw's name was the first on Charles I's death warrant and he was present when the royal head was cut off on 30th January 1649. John Bradshaw fulfilled the promise as a lad and did indeed perform an act "that all the world must wonder at".

The chapel, with the farm in the background

The Stockport Parish Register records one further act of vandalism. Across the birth certificate of John Bradshaw someone has scribbled the word TRAITOR. Those who walk close to Marple Hall's ruins should think about this place in history that is devoted to John Bradshaw.

10. Follow a steep path down to the right and then alongside the grounds of Marple Hall School. Here is an area close to the confluence with the Tame and the Goyt that has already absorbed the Etherow. Thus the Mersey's trio of tributaries are united.

11. The path descends to Dooley Lane and passes a garden centre to the right within which is a very pleasant little café area. Look over Otterspool Bridge to view the Goyt. This is a very pleasant spot but the road (the A627) is always busy. Obviously this stretch of the Goyt was once the haunt of the otter but this is not the case these days. Follow the busy road for a very short distance before turning right back to the Chadkirk Country Estate Car Park.

SECTION 2: THE MANCHESTER SHIP CANAL

Those seeking walks in attractive surroundings might not select a couple of strolls around the Manchester Ship Canal. This is, after all, very much a commercial waterway – but not exclusively so.

Anyone wishing to explore the catchment of the Mersey on foot, however, has to pay attention to the Ship Canal. Two aspects in particular need to be considered. Firstly, the canal's disruption of the river between Irlam and Warrington means that the canal and the Mersey now run together. Secondly, the fact the Mersey became one of the world's most industrialised rivers was largely due to the construction of canals of which the Ship Canal was by far the largest.

The Manchester Ship Canal has itself been the subject of several books and its 35½-mile (57km) length may not always be easy or attractive walking, but to industrial archaeologists, there are few areas more interesting. The two walks included here are not easy to map because Victorian industrialists knew that land was money and industries were built where land was available. Apart from Salford Quays and the Ellesmere Port Museum described here, other walks also pass close to the Ship Canal.

Another point to note is that industrial areas tend to change more regularly than more rural areas along the watercourses. These changes are obvious in the Salford Quays area (see walk 5) which has now become a tourist location. The Ellesmere Port area over the last century has been transformed by the construction of oil terminals and car production plants all of which demand efficient motorway and rail links (see walk 6).

All these areas must be explored if the Mersey catchment portrait is to be painted. Once the decision has been made to stroll in these places the rewards can be great indeed.

Walk 5: Ordsall and Salford Quays

Directions: From the M60 follow the M602 signed Salford. At the end of this road is a roundabout. The third exit is onto Trafford Road (A5063). Look for signs to Ordsall Hall where there is a free car park. As an alternative follow the A5063 and look for a right turn into the Quays and the Lowry Centre. Here there is a multi-storey car park. Payment obviously depends on how long you stay.

Public Transport: Salford Quays station is 1½ miles from the Lowry Centre. Metro link services also stops close to the Lowry. From Manchester Ordsall Hall can be reached via bus numbers 71, 73, 84 and 92. For bus times ring 0161 228 7811

Map Reference: OS Explorer 277 Grid Reference 816 966 Manchester A to Z (Page 85 Grid H6 and H7)

Distance: Around 4 miles.

Time: Hard to judge because there are so many essential stops involving visits. Allow at least 4 hours.

Note: Of all the strolls around the Mersey catchment this is the most difficult to map. The route crosses busy roads. Changes are also going on at some speed.

Mention Salford and many people still think of the industry associated with the old docks, warehouses and a confused jumble of waterways mainly created when the Manchester Ship Canal was built in the 1890s. This obtained its essential water by impounding the Irwell and its meander which once fed directly into the River Mersey.

At one time, there was a Heritage Centre on site and this published a trail through the then run-down docklands. At night this route was regarded as a criminal-infested no-go area. The construction of the Lowry Centre and the War Museum plus improvements in water quality led to old buildings being demolished or developed into up-market hotels, restaurants and housing. The Heritage Centre was closed in 1999 but its web site has remained open so that this slice of history can still be savoured [www.spectec.co.uk/salfordquays]

Things are changing all the time around this area and busy roads have to be carefully negotiated. In a very real sense, however, this is typical of the Mersey and its tributaries. One of the world's major industrial watercourses, the Mersey is a miracle of survival and full of breath-taking history. Amidst all this, wildlife survives. Spend time on the return along the Quays to observe the birds seen regularly but especially in winter, including heron, cormorant, pochard, tufted duck plus mute swans and other species.

Nearby are many fast food outlets such as McDonald's and Harry Ramsden's Fish and Chip shop. There are increasing numbers of good hotels. Close by are the Old Trafford Football and Cricket grounds. The football museum can be combined with the walk described here.

The Route

1. The confluence of the Irwell and the Mersey has disappeared forever. All trace of the Irwell as a tranquil trout and salmon stream surrounded by gracious buildings has been swamped. Or has it? Actually one gem of the old English countryside remains and has been restored. This is Ordsall Hall. The name comes from the Old English words 'ord' and 'halh' which together means a nook. This was accurate because it was once situated on a sweeping meander of the Irwell. This later proved to be a perfect site on which to construct the Manchester terminus of the Ship Canal.

Ordsall is first recorded in a legal document of 1177 and there was a substantial manor house on site by 1251. There was almost certainly a Roman settlement here and later a Saxon manor. In 1335 the Radclyffe family purchased Ordsall and it was they who made it important in both Lancashire's social and military history. By 1380 they had constructed a timber-framed house, which is the basis of the present hall.

There were 16th- and 17th-century additions and there are also suggestions that Ordsall was a meeting place for those who schemed the Gunpowder plot of 1605, which was an attempt to blow up Parliament along with James I. Robert Catesby was certainly related to the Radclyffes and Guy Fawkes himself is thought to have been briefed at Ordsall. Absolute proof is, however, lacking.

From the early 18th century, the hall and the Radclyffes seem to have fallen on hard times and the house was almost derelict for many years.

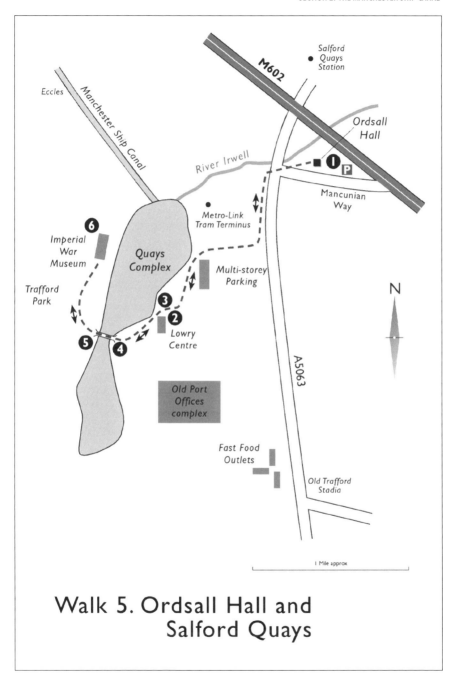

Walk 5. Ordsall Hall and Salford Quays

Ordsall Hall

Salford Corporation bought the hall in 1959 and after extensive work Ordsall was opened as a local history museum in 1972. It has gone from strength to strength ever since. It is open daily except Saturdays, there is no fee and details of exhibitions can be found by ringing 0161 872 0251, fax 0161 872 4951.

A Victorian farmhouse kitchen has been laid out in what was the actual kitchen at Ordsall from at least 1639. There are displays of pewter and horn utensils, which were used prior to pottery. The pottery industry only prospered when canals ensured the smooth transportation of very delicate merchandise.

Time should also be spent in looking closely at the exterior of the hall, which really is a refreshing blast from the past. Look also for a stretch of the Irwell which is still navigable for barges, and which now supports fish.

2. From Ordsall cross the very busy road system and follow signs to Salford Quays. Then follow the signs to the Lowry Centre. Ordsall is ancient, but the Lowry is a magnificent modern structure.

Glass and metal combine as the architectural theme of the Lowry, which opened on 28th April 2000 and quite rightly is the showpiece of the modern docklands area. As in this walk, however, an effort must be made to view the Lowry and Ordsall as part of the same historical jigsaw.

The Lowry (free admission) has something for everyone. There are seating areas, bars and cafés with views over the Quays. Art exhibitions (all free, donations welcome) celebrate the life of L.S. Lowry (1887-1976), the Salford artist who painted the famous 'matchstick' men. Two theatres seat 1,730 and 466, and there is a gift shop with a well-appointed book section. Tel: 0870 787 5780; fax: 0161 876 2021.

3. From the Lowry, follow the route down to the docks and stroll around these landscaped areas. Look out on the dockside for a piece of engineering looking like a giant refrigerator.

The Manchester Ship Canal was rightly regarded as heavily polluted, even by Mersey standards. Gradually work by the Environment Agency, industry (including United Utilities) and the closure of some factories, which caused less effluent to be discharged, all led to improvements in water quality. Fish and birds began to return and on-going work by these bodies and the splendid Mersey Basin Campaign, accelerated the improvement in water quality in the Quays. This led to building investment including the Lowry and the War Museum.

In the 1990s, APEM Ltd (an aquatic science company based in Manchester) came up with a revolutionary scheme to accelerate the improvements on what is best described as a "long-term but temporary" research project. In its simplest form, the apparatus seen on the Quays bubbles oxygen into the water, especially during periods of hot weather when oxygen levels are low. This was the first such development in the world. Its success along with other clean-ups meant that the docks are used to host the swimming section of Triathlon events, including the Manchester Commonwealth Games of 2002.

4. This is the place to sit on one of the many seats and think about the history of the Manchester Ship Canal. From the tidal reach of the Mersey near Eastham (see walk 24) the canal runs some 36 miles to Salford Quays and passes through five locks. The cut is unique in

Barges on the Irwell

Britain in that it is a seaway with docks all along its routes. It is also a massive harbour. It was opened by Queen Victoria in 1894 and the cost of the seven-year construction was a then-massive £14,350,000. Costs went considerably over budget and, in view of present-day engineering projects, it is easy to say that there is nothing new in this.

The Ship Canal was built to link to other already existing canals including the Shropshire Union at Ellesmere Port (see walk 6).

5. Continue from the Lowry area along a walkway and over the splendid Millennium footbridge. Look over the bridge and look at The Trafford Park complex. Here is yet another site of world importance.

Before the construction of the Ship Canal, the Irwell flowed between the twin cities of Manchester and Salford before meandering through the countryside around Trafford Park, Barton and Davyhulme. Then just to the south of Flixton the Irwell merged with the Mersey.

Once the Ship Canal was complete, Trafford Hall and Park were sold and the grounds of the old manor developed into the first Industrial Trading Site in the world. Exports and imports were easily linked to the sea and thence to the ports of the world.

6. The Imperial War Museum's Salford outpost (tel: 0161 836 4000) should be regarded as a triumph for many reasons. It is one of few enterprises that came in under budget. The architect Daniel Liberskind estimated the cost to be £40 million, but lottery funding was refused. More recently Liberskind won the commission to design the Ground Zero site in New York. The War Museum plans were altered slightly and the eventual cost was reduced to £28.5 million. The original plan was to have an auditorium but this was postponed, although it is still hoped that this can eventually be developed.

The Manchester area, and especially the Salford Docks, took a terrible beating by German bombers in World War II and this is rightly celebrated by a 55 metre (180ft) vertical spire. This is close to the entrance and there is a 30 metre (100ft) gallery from which the Manchester skyline can be viewed. Here is a balance between a local, national and international museum using relevant artefacts as well as the latest touch-button technology. The Museum was voted the North West Visitor Attraction of the Year for 2003 and entry is free.

Walk 6: Ellesmere Port

Directions: The Ellesmere Port Boat Museum is very close to Junction 9 of the M53. There is clear signing to and off the motorway. The parking at the Museum is excellent and well signed.

Public Transport: The Museum is within strolling distance of Ellesmere Port railway station. Buses run from Chester and Birkenhead. Number C3 is the best.

Map Reference: OS Explorer 266 Grid Reference 410 775

Distance: This is difficult to state accurately because the museum site is being developed and the walk changes as it twists, turns and crosses bridges. Alas there is no walking route leaflet in print at the moment but the area is wheelchair friendly. There is even a tactile trail for the poorly sighted.

Time: around 3½ miles will be covered and at least four hours should be allowed.

Before the Canal Age, there was no such place as Ellesmere Port and on the shoreline of the Mersey was the tiny fishing and farming village of Whitby. Its population was only around 200. In medieval times these souls could look out to Stanlow Abbey, which was established by the Cistercians in 1178. The monks found the going tough on the edge of the Mersey marshes and in 1296 they removed to drier lands at Whalley close to the confluence of the rivers Calder and Ribble near Clitheroe. Whitby, however, was left in peace until the coming first of the Shropshire Union Canal and then the giant Manchester Ship Canal.

In 1793 an Act of Parliament allowed a canal to be cut linking the River Severn near Shrewsbury to the Mersey and thence to the sea. Work proceeded so quickly that the "Shroppie" opened to traffic in 1795. This meant that the industries based in the Cheshire town of Ellesmere had their own port and hence named it Ellesmere Port. This canal is 66½ miles (107 km) long and has 46 locks. The development of the port meant an increase in work opportunities and therefore population but this was not without considerable environmental impact. This accelerated quickly as the Manchester Ship Canal was built.

The concept of linking Manchester directly to the sea and thus removing the large landing fees demanded by Liverpool developed as early as the mid-18th century.

Ellesmere Port Boat Museum

The Manchester Ship became known as the "Peoples' Canal" because it was built by money generated by 39,000 private investors. The project was divided into sections and each had its own workforce and equipment. In 1888 the Eastham (see walk 24) to Ellesmere Port section employed 1,000 men living in shanty towns. Although they used a few locomotives and steam driven excavators most of the 53 million tons of mud, soil and rock involved human muscle operating shovels and wheelbarrows. This spoil was used to build banks to ensure that the Ship Canal and the Mersey were kept separate.

The Route

1. From the car park, you should first visit the Boat Museum. This is open daily from April to October but in the cooler months it is closed on Thursday and Friday. Telephone: 0151 355 5017

   This is very much a hands-on museum and there is plenty to see around the 7.5 acre (3 hectare) site. There is a shop, café, archive centre and library plus a well-appointed Conference facility. This is the place to study the work of Thomas Telford who was born in 1757 near Dumfries. Lots of his canal architecture remains despite a devastating fire in 1970. By the time Telford died in 1834 he had virtually written a canal history on his own.

Here is splendid Georgian architecture especially the tollhouse. Ellesmere Port underwent major developments from mid-Victorian times up to and during the First World War. Thereafter there was a decline and the complex virtually ceased to function by the 1950s. In the 1960s volunteers initiated the Boat Museum Trust which still runs the museum.

2. From the car park follow the track down to the banks of the Ship Canal. Look closely at this area because until 1894 when the cut opened the Victorians regarded this as a safe bathing beach. Look to the right and see the massive Stanlow oil terminal.

This has all but obliterated what little remained of Stanlow Abbey. The network of pipes and the burning oil-based fumes are not popular with people but because people are not popular with birds Stanlow has proved to be a haven for wildlife. Shell, for example, commissioned an ecological report of their site and it makes encouraging reading. The list includes little ringed plover, kingfisher, kestrel, house martin, peregrine falcon, stonechat and many others whilst stoat and fox are common.

3. Turn away from Stanlow and follow the towpath keeping the Ship Canal to the right. Beyond this is the tidal estuary of the Mersey and the river itself. To the left is the site of the old gas works. This was built by the Shropshire Union and Railway Company in 1863. The railway companies realised very early in the development that canals were still a threat to their business and bought up shares predictably leading

Birds such as this kestrel, soon adapt to industrial areas

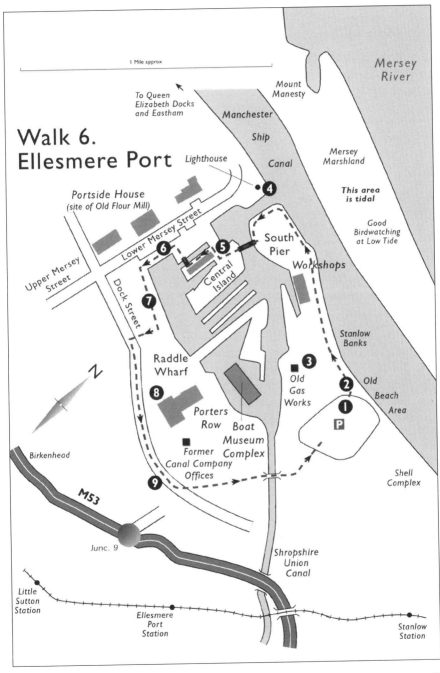

1 Mile approx

Mersey
River

Mount
Manesty

To Queen
Elizabeth Docks
and Eastham

Manchester

Walk 6.
Ellesmere Port

Ship

Lighthouse

Canal

Mersey
Marshland

Portside House
(site of Old Flour Mill)

Lower Mersey Street

4

This area
is tidal

Good
Birdwatching
at Low Tide

South
Pier

6

5

Upper Mersey
Street

Central
Island

Workshops

Dock Street

7

Stanlow
Banks

Raddle
Wharf

8

3

Old
Gas
Works

2

1

P

Old
Beach
Area

Birkenhead

Porters
Row Boat
Museum
Former Complex
Canal Company
Offices

9

Shell
Complex

M53

Junc. 9

Shropshire
Union
Canal

Little
Sutton
Station

Ellesmere
Port
Station

Stanlow
Station

to take-overs. The self-contained gas works first illuminated the docks and then the associated residential blocks.

4. Continue along the towpath passing the craft workshops on the left. Continue to the entrance from the Ship Canal into the dock complex and the Shropshire Union Canal link. Look out on the opposite bank to the lighthouse and Mount Manesty. The lighthouse is no longer in use but in the days of sailing ships it guided vessels from the main channel of the Mersey into the busy docks.

In the distance is Mount Manesty, which is the largest of the bunds of excavated earth (protective embankments) piled up to separate the canal from the Mersey. Why Mount Manesty? Because the engineer in charge of this section of the construction was called Manesty! Beyond this are the Queen Elizabeth Docks at Eastham (see walk 24). These were built in 1954 and were designed to load and discharge bulk liquid petroleum products and edible oils. Here is the largest enclosed dock system in the UK. The Boat Museum is an historical sandwich between the docks and the Stanlow oil complex!

5. From the south pier area turn left keeping the dock area to the right. Turn sharp right over a bridge and onto the area known as Central Island. It was this area which was most damaged during the fire of 1970 and some of Telford's warehouses were destroyed. These were built because goods had to be transhipped between small barges and much larger ocean-going ships. One building lost was the arched warehouse, which allowed goods to be moved between a high and low basin, but thankfully the lower arches can still be seen.

Look to the left where there is one remaining china clay warehouse. This clay was brought by sea from Cornwall and then transported by barges to the Potteries. The finished ceramics were carried in the reverse direction and provided employment for the Mersey workers.

6. Turn right over another footbridge onto the dockside and left into Lower Mersey Street. Look to the right to see the old mechanism, which was used to operate the locks. Here too is the splendid little lock-keeper's cottage, which is a listed building.

There is much to see in this area and lots of time should be allowed especially as the Museum is always evolving. Look out for a splendid set of Georgian-style cottages overlooking the canal port. These were constructed by the Shropshire Union Canal Company to house their senior staff. Portside House stands on the site of a flour mill dating to the time that grain was milled and exported from the docks.

On the left of Lower Mersey Street is the old entrance to the "Mill Arm" of the canal. Milling at Ellesmere was important from the beginning of the 20th century to around 1970 when newer, larger and better equipped plants were built in other areas of Merseyside.

7. Continue along Lower Mersey Street and then left onto Raddle Wharf. Here can be seen reminders of the railway age. Look for bumps on the road surface, which show the position of the old railway tracks and the site of two turntables. These date from the days when the port had a substantial business dealing in iron ore in one direction and manufactured pig iron to outlets far beyond the Mersey.

8. From Raddle Wharf turn right and then left onto Dock Street. On the left is Porters Row. Lots of time should be spent here especially the area facing the dock complex and the Shropshire Union Canal.

At Porters Row visitors are often greeted by an informative lady guide dressed in Victorian garb. The workers' dwellings have been restored and there is often a roaring fire and a black leaded range.

Aspidistra plants are on display and it is pointed out that these plants thrived in parlours as they were not affected either by the fumes from coal fires or by gaslight.

There is a privy outside and nervous visitors should be prepared for the fact that this is "occupied" by a dummy. There is also an old pigsty and a "working" chicken coup. On the walls are lots of colourful metal adverts including a number for Sunlight soap (see walk 25).

9. From Porters Row return to Dock Street. Turn left and pass the old canal company offices on the left. Continue along Dock Street to the car park.

SECTION 3: THE BOLLIN

Although it has had to cope with some industry, and later with the Manchester Airport complex, the Bollin catchment has always been quite rural, affording some truly inspiring scenery and making it 'strolling country' par excellence.

In soggy uplands of Lancashire, Cheshire and Derbyshire rise two streams, the Bollin and the Dean. Once merged, it is the Dean that loses its identity and the Bollin then flows on to its union with the Manchester Ship Canal and the Mersey.

Around the Bollin are accessible reservoirs, country parks and the historic settlements of Macclesfield, Prestbury, Wilmslow, Styal Country Park, Quarry Bank Mill, Pigley stairs and Dunham Massey house and estate. At Quarry Bank and Dunham Massey, the National Trust has played a major role in the preservation of industrial sites surrounded by attractive walking routes.

My choice of the two Bollin walks obviously had to be selective but I wanted to concentrate on how the Bollin coped with industry at Styal (walk 7). Dunham Massey (walk 8) is a fine example of how a stately home refused to allow industry to intrude and even managed to soften the environmental impact caused by the construction of the Bridgewater Canal.

Walk 7: Styal Country Park and Quarry Bank Mill

Directions: From the M56 follow the signs towards Manchester Airport. Large brown signs off the motorway at Junction 6 indicate Quarry Bank Mill. Take care around the Airport Terminals complex as the brown signs to Quarry Bank disappear. At a roundabout follow the signs for Cheadle (B5166). Continue to Styal when the clear brown signs appear again. A right turn leads into the car park. There is a fee to enter the National Trust property; tel: 01625 527468.

Public Transport: There is a train service to Wilmslow. Bus service No 200 leads to Styal Country Park. There is a bus shelter in the car park and times are displayed on a weatherproof board.

Map Reference: OS Explorer 268 Grid Reference 832 835

Distance: 4 miles

Time: Allow 3 hours and more if you wish to enter Quarry Bank Mill.

This walk along the River Bollin is focussed around Samuel Greg's Quarry Bank Mill, which was built in 1784. It produced cotton until 1959 and is now run as a working museum by the National Trust. Any portrait of the Mersey and its tributaries cannot afford to miss this combination of river scenery and industrial archaeology.

The original power for the mill was the River Bollin, which is a substantial stream in its own right, but just before the mill its flow is supplemented by the River Dean. The two watercourses meet at the well-named Twinnies Bridge. An old word 'Twistle' actually means a confluence or a boundary. Prior to the development of the cotton mill, both of these rivers had water-powered corn mills and there are records of these dating from 1335. Although not relevant today, there are still old references such as 'higher' and 'lower' mill fields on the Bollin.

The area has been occupied at least since Saxon times and Styal has coped with intrusions very well from the time of the Gregs. A further disruption caused by the expansion of Manchester International Airport has been well handled. Any portrait of the Mersey cannot afford to miss this combination of river scenery and industrial archaeology.

47

The Route

1. From the car park descend a gentle slope and find an information board close to a wooden hut. On display is a request by the local nature wardens asking visitors to record their sightings of fauna and flora. It is to be hoped that these will eventually result in an illustrated leaflet, which will add interest to a rich wildlife area. Descend a steep winding path, which sweeps first right and then left as it meets a narrow road leading to Quarry Bank Mill.

2. Look left and take time to explore the mill complex and enjoy a snack or for those who want to eat in luxury there is a restaurant. There are toilets and the shop is stocked with books, gifts and publications relating to the history of the Mill.

The complex of mill buildings is in good repair and a tour of the mill follows the history of Greg's empire from waterwheel, water turbine and steam-operated machinery. On most days, the machinery operates, to the delight of the school parties that use Quarry Bank as part of their curriculum. There is an accurate chronological history of the cotton industry as it developed around the river catchment. In the summer of 2003, a reconstruction of a mill manager's office opened to the public. After watching the machines at work, those interested can buy a sample of Quarry Bank Mill cotton from the shop.

3. Leave the office and café on the left and continue ahead. Look to the right and see the Jubilee Playground opened to celebrate the Queen's Golden Jubilee. Look down to the right and see (and hear) the crashing waters of the Bollin Weir. This was built to increase the power of the river when water was the power source.

4. Continue on and cross a footbridge. The river is on the right and a substantial pond on the left. This once held a reserve water supply used when the river ran dry in times of low rainfall. These days the pond is a haven for waterfowl and an ideal place to enjoy natural history at all times of year. When cotton was produced using water power it was more in balance with nature than in the days of steam. Initially, as at Styal, cotton mills were sited in the countryside but once steam took over huge towns could be developed. Population, productivity and profit combined to produce pollution.

5. Bear left around the pond unless you want to extend the walk along

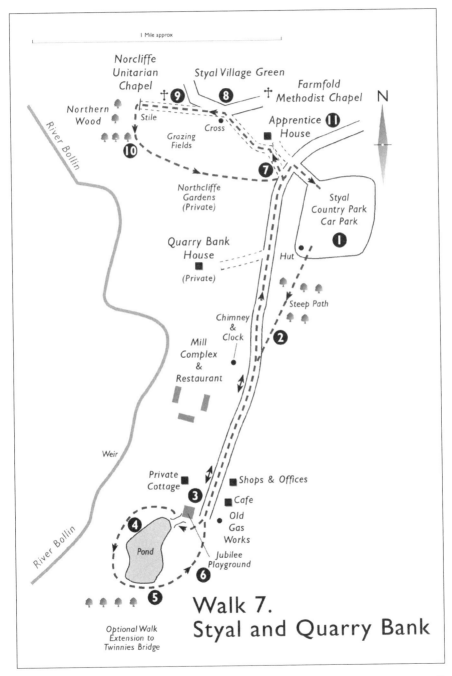

I Mile approx

Norcliffe Unitarian Chapel

Styal Village Green

Farmfold Methodist Chapel

N

Northern Wood

Stile

Cross

Apprentice House

Grazing Fields

Northcliffe Gardens (Private)

Styal Country Park Car Park

Quarry Bank House

Hut

(Private)

Steep Path

Chimney & Clock

Mill Complex & Restaurant

Weir

Private Cottage

Shops & Offices

Cafe

Old Gas Works

Pond

Jubilee Playground

River Bollin

River Bollin

Optional Walk Extension to Twinnies Bridge

Walk 7.
Styal and Quarry Bank

the Bollin to Twinnies Bridge and then retrace your steps. Pass through an interesting area of woodland. Now the Jubilee Playground is on the left.

6. On the right is a circular wall behind which is the remnant of the gasworks associated with the mills. The Gregs were enlightened employers for their time but they had a keen eye for profit. Gas production was not cheap but its light allowed a shift system to operate over 24 hours instead of less than eight in winter.

Styal Mill: chimney and clock

From the gasworks, stroll through the mills and pass the clock tower and chimney and then along the road with Quarry Bank House on the left. This has been a private residence since it was constructed for Samuel Greg in 1797.

7. Ascend the steep road and look for a sign to the left indicating Styal Village. This grassy footpath reveals the garden of the Apprentice House on the right (see point 11). To the left is a field with cattle grazing on it in season, much as would have been the case before Styal Mill was built.

8. Pass through a set of metal gates and reach Styal village, which was important in medieval times. Here is an ancient cross that once stood on Styal Green until it was relocated following a motor accident in 1981. To the right and left are chapels with Farm Fold Methodist Chapel to the right. Straight ahead is the unspoiled village green surrounded by pretty cottages.

9. Turn left and follow the footpath to the 18th-century Norcliffe Unitarian Chapel. Enjoy this attractive building before continuing ahead to a stile.

Norcliffe Unitarian Chapel

10. Cross this stile and enter Northern Woods. Take the left fork and ignore a wooden footbridge built in 1995 to celebrate the centenary of the National Trust. Approach an information board. Turn left and follow an obvious footpath. Meet a crossroads indicating Northcliffe Gardens (a private house) and signed to the right. Continue straight ahead and follow the footpath.

11. The footpath bears left, then right before meeting a road. Turn left to the Apprentice House. The garden has been planted in 19th-century style with herbs and fruit tended in the traditional manner.

The white-painted Apprentice House can be visited as part of Quarry Bank Mill entry fee. This was built in 1790 to provide accommodation for up to 100 children who were 'obtained' from workhouses. Present-day critics suggest that to treat children as working chattels was inhuman. So it was – but Greg provided them with food, clothes and they were taught to read and write. Thus, they were better off than most children who had to work in coal mines and town-based mills (see walk 3) – at least these children could breathe fresh air as they walked to and from work.

The walk concludes by returning along the short track from the Apprentice's House to the car park and the bus stop.

Walk 8: Dunham Massey and the Bollin

Directions: Take the M56 towards Manchester Airport. At Junction 7 follow a brown sign indicating Dunham Massey. Dunham Park is open every day (an extensive car park requires payment) whilst the house and gardens are open between April and October each day except Fridays. There are good facilities for the disabled. In the old coach house is an audio-visual display, which relates the history of the estate and associated families; tel: 0161 941 1025.

Public Transport: There is a regular bus service to Dunham Town, which is in easy walking distance of Dunham Massey.

Map Reference: OS Explorer 268 Grid Reference 735 870

Distance: 3½ miles

Time: 2 hours

This stretch of the River Bollin has, thankfully, been dominated by the estate of Dunham Massey for centuries. In the 18th century, the Bridgewater Canal sliced its way through the Bollin Valley.

Dunham Massey was first mentioned in 1323 but the present house was built in 1732 for George Booth who was descended from the first owner, Hamon de Massey. From the Masseys the estate passed into the hands of the Grey family whose most famous member was the tragic Lady Jane Grey (1537-1554). Jane became Queen of England in 1553. She had a valid claim because she was a Protestant, whilst Mary Tudor was a firm Catholic. Only a few days after Lady Jane was deposed, Mary still saw her as a threat and signed her death warrant. There is no doubt that Jane Grey was the Queen from 19th July to 22nd August 1553 but she did not live long enough to be crowned. Her portrait is on display at Dunham Massey Hall.

The Route

1. From Dunham Massey car park follow the signs to the house and beyond this the deer park, which occupies around 230 acres (92 hectares). This is the place to spend time and look out for the remnant of a motte on Castle Hill overlooking the Bollin near the junction of the A56 with the A556.

The herd of fallow deer is a real feature, although experts feel that

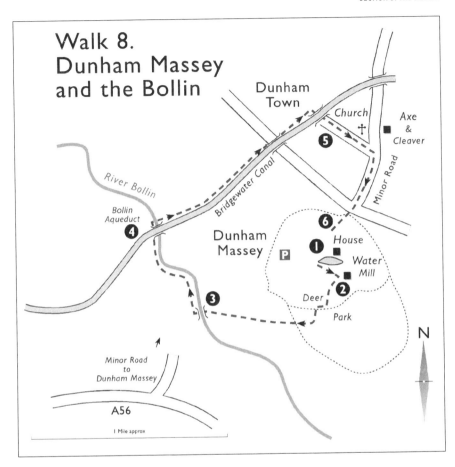

Walk 8.
Dunham Massey
and the Bollin

the species is not native but was introduced by the Normans (some also suggest Roman introductions). There were extensive imports by Tudor and Victorian landowners. Herds such as the one at Dunham Massey are long established and the large palmate-shaped antlers are an easily identified feature.

2. Also in the grounds is an impressively restored water mill. This was built in 1616 to grind corn but in 1860 it was adapted to function as a sawmill. This was not commercially successful and was closed in 1895. It has recently been restored.

3. Follow an obvious track leading first downhill and then crossing the Bollin and sweeping right. Pass through low-lying meadows to the Bollin aqueduct.

The old water mill, Dunham Massey

4. The aqueduct carries the Bridgewater Canal over the River Bollin. On April 2, 1971 the stretch close to the aqueduct began to leak and eventually burst. Great damage resulted around the immediate area but there was a dramatic knock-on effect. There are no locks on the main line and water levels were affected as far as Manchester some ten miles away.

In the 1970s, canals were not considered to be important and the repair was largely the result of pressure from the specially formed Bridgewater Canal Trust. We owe a lot to these locally formed pressure groups (see walk 4). A careful look down from the aqueduct area still reveals the effect of the burst.

5. From the aqueduct follow the canal towpath keeping the Bridgewater on the right. Cross a road bridge and pass into a village which is actually called Dunham Town. Here are some old cottages, the small parish church of St Mark and a good pub called the Axe and Cleaver. At the church turn right and follow the road to Dunham Park.

6. Enter the courtyard and old stable block of the hall. Here, there is a café and a well-stocked gift and craft shop. Take time to explore the house built on the medieval site by the Second Earl of Warrington around 1730. The National Trust has done a fine job and the site is attractive with ponds, a splendid orangery and, of course, the deer.

During the construction of the Bridgewater Canal the labourers used the Bollin as a fishery, which was then "full of salmon". Apart from the aqueduct area the Bridgewater did not affect the Bollin, but the fact that it did not was certainly due to the Dunham Massey family.

The construction of the Manchester Ship Canal, however, was much more of a problem. For a long stretch between Irlam and Bollin Point the Ship Canal and the Mersey are one and the same. It was obviously easier, and therefore cheaper, for the canal engineers to use a straight section of the river rather than cut a new channel.

Just beyond Warburton, the River Bollin now flows into the Ship Canal and its original confluence with the Mersey has been lost. Close to the junction with the Ship Canal at Bollin Point the Mersey leaves the Ship Canal and follows its original course then flows on towards Warrington.

SECTION 4: THE BRIDGEWATER CANAL

Serious canal historians will argue over which was the first canal to be built in England. Most would say that the accolade should be given to the Bridgewater but in recent years an increasing number of enthusiasts insist that the St Helens Canal should be regarded as the first (see walk 20 and 21).

No account of the Mersey should omit a study of the Bridgewater and the St Helens canals as both link to the river. The walker should also enjoy exploring their towpaths, which pass through some areas of idyllic countryside whilst still showing the signs of industrial impact.

The Bridgewater is an example of a contour canal that sticks to a line 25.2 metres (83ft) above sea level and thus avoids the need for expensive lock construction. The length of the main line of the canal is 37km (23 miles and 3 furlongs) but later, other branches added a further 26.4km (16 miles and 3 furlongs).

The next four walks set the Bridgewater and its link into the Leeds and Liverpool in context but the Walk 8 (Dunham Mersey) also impacts on the Bridgewater.

Walk 9: Along the Bridgewater – Worsley

Directions: From the M61 and M60, turn off at Junction 14. Take care to negotiate two roundabouts. Follow the signs towards Swinton (A575). Just into Worsley, find a car park on the right.

Public Transport: There are buses to Worsley from both Swinton and Manchester in one direction and to Leigh and Bolton in the other direction.

Map Reference: OS Explorer 276 and 277 Grid Reference 752 019

Distance: Allow 6 miles if all diversions are taken.

Time: Allow 3 hours.

Over the last two to three hundred years, the Mersey catchment has been managed to serve the needs of the Industrial Revolution. Nowhere is this more evident than in the Worsley area. Here the origins of the Bridgewater Canal can be explored. The once-quiet hamlet became a hub of heavy industry and is now almost but not quite strangled by one of the busiest motorway junctions in Britain.

As Manchester developed from a village into what amounted to an expanding 'cottonopolis', waterpower was replaced by steam. The production of steam required water and coal and transporting the latter was expensive. The Duke of Bridgewater had vast coal deposits, literally beneath his country seat at Worsley, and he hit on the idea of constructing a water corridor to Manchester. He was also smart enough to realise that, if he continued his cut to the Mersey estuary, he could open up a lucrative import and export market. In time, he produced an income from the three 'c's – coal, cotton and canal.

The Route

1. From the car park turn away from Worsley and negotiate the often horrendous roundabouts. Use the left-hand pavement towards Leigh and Bolton and look to the left. At a complex of hotels and a golf course, turn to the left and approach Worsley Old Hall – once the home of the Duke of Bridgewater, and now the perfect place for morning coffee or a spot of lunch; tel: 0161 799 5015. In the late

Worsley Packet House

1990s, the whole area was in a sad state of repair but a thorough restoration has recently taken place. The old Duke would now be proud of the place.

2. The Old Hall was an important family home for the Egertons from Elizabethan times but, when the canal was being planned, the building was used for accommodation and offices. At the same time, the first Duke built a new hall of red brick. Those staying at one of the hotels on the old site and perhaps enjoying a leisurely meal or a round of golf should take the time to absorb the history of this place and give thanks for its survival.

3. Return from the Old Hall and find the church of St Mark across the busy road. Whilst the Canal Duke would recognise his halls this church with its spire would be a new experience for him. His successor the first Earl of Ellesmere rebuilt the old parish church in 1846. This is sited on the steep hill called Worsley Brow, which then overlooked the village. This view is now almost obscured by the motorway developments.

The new church is a fine example of the work of Sir George Gilbert Scott. Some of the furnishings, however, would be recognised by the Old Duke including the pulpit and organ screens imported from France and Flanders and dating from the 16th and 17th centu-

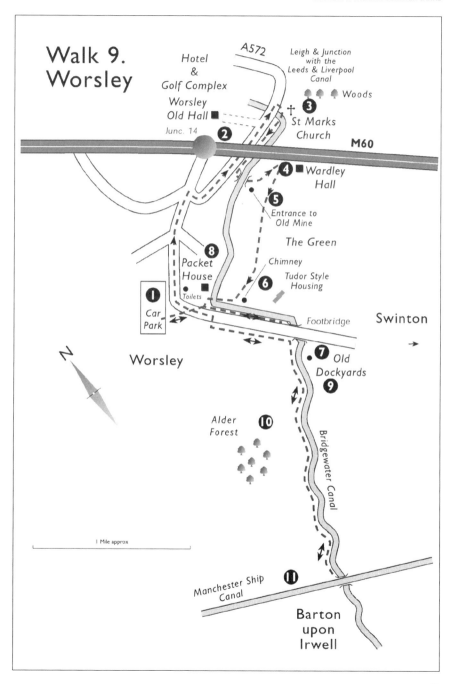

Walk 9.
Worsley

A572

Hotel
&
Golf Complex

Leigh & Junction
with the
Leeds & Liverpool
Canal

Woods

Worsley
Old Hall ■

Junc. 14 ❷

† ❸
St Marks
Church

M60

Junc. 14

❹ ■ Wardley
Hall

Entrance to
Old Mine

The Green

❺

❽
Packet
House

Chimney

Tudor Style
Housing ❻

❶
Car
Park

Toilets ■

Footbridge

Swinton

Worsley

❼ Old
Dockyards
❾

Alder
Forest ❿

Bridgewater Canal

I Mile approx

↔

❶❶

Manchester Ship
Canal

Barton
upon
Irwell

ries. I do not know what he would have made of his predecessor's tomb, which dominates the interior. The first Lord Ellesmere never did anything without lots of pomp and pride.

4. Perhaps because they do not expect to find nature so close to motorways, visitors often miss the joys of Worsley Woods. These were also largely the work of the First Lord Ellesmere. In the woodland area, he created footpaths, an artificial lake, which he stocked with fish and he even had a shooting lodge which he called his aviary.

Also, look out for the Ellesmere memorial, which many think was built to celebrate the canal builder. In fact, it was completed in 1859 as another memorial to Francis Edgerton the First Earl of Ellesmere. The monument is surrounded by housing and is best viewed from a distance with binoculars.

5. Wardley Hall is worth a diversion and is too often missed by walkers. Those who do visit sometimes confuse it with Worsley Old Hall. Wardley Hall dates from the 16th century and is now the residence of the Roman Catholic Bishop of Salford.

The hall is the last resting-place of the skull of Ambrose Barlow, who was a Catholic priest during the turbulent early years of the 17th century. Pope Paul decided to make Father Ambrose a Saint as late as 1970. Ambrose Barlow became a priest in 1604 and a year later, many Lancastrian Catholics were implicated in the plot to blow up James I whilst opening Parliament in 1605 (see walk 5). Father Ambrose was beloved by the Downes family who lived at Wardley Hall. He worked fearlessly to provide Lancashire people with the Mass and spent many years hiding in priest holes around the county. On Easter Sunday 1641, the Vicar of Leigh caught his arch-enemy and Ambrose was sent to Lancaster Castle to be hanged, drawn and quartered. His head was carried in secret to Wardley Hall where it has rested ever since.

5. From Wardley Hall retrace the route and bear left into Worsley. Divert to the right and look to the right over the mine entrance of the canal. This was a triumph for one of the unsung canal engineers, John Gilbert – who has been belatedly remembered in the name of a local pub. Everyone knows of James Brindley but Gilbert was just as important in the annals of the Bridgewater.

Gilbert cut some 46 miles of tunnels into mines, which delved deep into the ground towards Leigh and allowed some of the shafts to flood. Coal was then brought straight from the coalface to stocks held in the village, via very basic barges. These were so simple that some of their timbers stuck out. This gave them the name of starvation barges. A close look into the waters of the mine opening will reveal the remains of submerged starvation barges.

A look at the red colour of this area of the canal suggests pollution. All coalmines are loaded with iron salts that dissolve in water and, when exposed to the air, they oxidise and the run-off becomes rust-red. This is not poisonous and the Bridgewater still supports enough fish to encourage anglers.

6. From the mine entrance return to the village and stroll to the right onto what seems to be a village green dating from Tudor times. How wrong can you be?

> *A lofty column breathing smoke*
> *Did I the builder's glory once inspire*
> *Whose founder was the Duke who far and wide*
> *Bridged water through Bridgewater's countryside*

The fountain on the 'village green' was once a red-brick chimney, which carried smoke away from the Duke of Bridgewater's coal yard. It carries the Latin inscription, which is translated above.

The centre of Worsley looks like a Tudor village but the houses were actually built around 1900. It is difficult to imagine that this area was once one of the busiest and dirtiest in the world.

7. From the chimney on the green, approach a solid-looking metal bridge. Look right and left over the bridge. There in the rusty water are colourful barges and to the right is one of the most attractive buildings to be found anywhere on the Bridgewater Canal.

8. Turn right and divert to the old Packet House. This is another building which some confuse with Worsley Old Hall. It was built in the late 18th century as a number of separate buildings. In 1845, the Tudor frontage was added on the orders of the First Earl of Ellesmere. The steps of the Packet House were used by travellers who walked down into the comfort of packet boats, which carried them into the heart of Manchester. Some then continued on to Warrington, Runcorn and to the Mersey itself.

The Bridgewater Canal and the Packet House

9. Return along the towpath from the Packet House, pass the Bridgewater Hotel on the right and the footbridge on the left. Keep to the left bank of the canal and look over the water to the historic boatyards. These were built in the 1760s and have changed very little since. These are the oldest such buildings to be found anywhere in England and it is good to see that they still function as boat repair yards.

10. Continue to follow the towpath towards Manchester and look left and right to marvel at the urban sprawl, with just a touch of the countryside through which the Bridgewater was once cut. Another Latin inscription at the base of the Worsley chimney stresses this combination:

Alas that I who gazed o'er field and town
Should to these base proportions dwindle down
But all's not over, still enough remains
To testify past glories, duties place

To the right of the towpath is an area known as Alder Forest, which is exactly what it once was. From medieval times alder trees were harvested. The wood was cut into the clog soles, which for centuries provided lanky lads and lasses with solid footwear.

The Barton Aqueduct

11. Continue along the towpath to reach the Barton swing aqueduct one of the most magnificent feats of Victorian engineering but one which needs to be placed in context.

Many claim that James Brindley was the architect – but this is not true. When the Bridgewater Canal was first built Brindley constructed an aqueduct to carry the cut over the River Irwell. Then, when the Manchester Ship Canal was built, Brindley's aqueduct was too low to allow high-masted vessels to pass. A new aqueduct was built to carry one canal (the Bridgewater) over another (the Ship Canal). A moveable section some 330 feet long (100 metres) was built and filled with water. When vessels were not passing through the Ship Canal the Bridgewater section was swung into its normal position, allowing the latter to function normally. The Barton Aqueduct is regarded as one of "the seven wonders of the Canal Age" and another is the Anderton Boat Lift (see walk 22).

From the aqueduct, the route to Worsley should be reversed but, on the return, time should be taken to explore the rich fauna and flora on this stretch of the canal. As the canal crosses the main road, follow the pavement past the Bridgewater Hotel and return to the car park.

Walk 10: Pennington Flash

Directions: The Flash is well signed from the A580 and situated just about one mile from the centre of Leigh. The main entrance is signed off the A572, and the Information Centre is reached along a well-maintained track lined with traffic calmers. There is a spacious car park near the Information Centre and there is usually a mobile snack bar.

Public Transport: There are several routes that stop close to the park. No 559 Leigh to Billinge. No 557 Leigh to Wigan. No 652 Leigh to Warrington. No 581 Bolton to Newton.

Map Reference: OS Explorer 276 Grid Reference 635 990

Distance: 4½ miles

Time: Allow 2½ to 3 hours and more if you are a keen naturalist.

This walk is essential for those who wish to look at the Mersey catchment in detail. In this present volume, space is at a premium and there is only one walk featuring the Leeds and Liverpool Canal. Even then, the stretch that runs close to Pennington Flash is only a link between the Bridgewater and the Leeds and Liverpool.

The purpose of the 127¼-mile canal was to link the Mersey estuary with the Humber estuary via Leeds.

Why then is there only this brief reference to the Leeds and Liverpool? The main reason is that major developments are in hand at the Mersey end, with British Waterways determined to improve access and to provide safer walking. These plans were already well in hand when it was announced that Liverpool had been selected as European City of Culture in 2008. This is also likely to improve the canal corridor and many fascinating strolls will be developed. At this stage, the Leeds and Liverpool would warrant a volume all to itself.

The Country Park was opened in April 1981 with the 170-acre (68-hectare) flash itself being surrounded by around 1000 acres (400 hectares) of varied habitat including a Municipal golf course.

At one time, the whole of this area was devoted to farming with its water supply coming from Hey Brook. Then coal was discovered and the present flash is mainly a result of mining subsidence.

The Route

1. The Information Centre is set amidst a complex, which includes toilets and access to the golf course. The Wardens are always on hand and are keen naturalists. The daily bird sightings are listed on a chalkboard and so are other interesting observations.

Note: The Country Park is developing all the time and new footpaths, hides, bird stations and other improvements are on-going. Telephone the Rangers office on **01942 605253.**

2. From the Information Centre meander along the path away from the car park and stroll between a number of ponds fringed by trees. The Flash itself is now an important angling venue (for day tickets apply at the Information Centre). These smaller ponds are used as stock ponds. The fish populations are regularly censused in consultation with the Environment Agency.

Fish are removed and used to restock the Flash and other locations and I have been lucky enough to watch the netting process on several occasions. Prize specimens of roach, tench, bream, perch and very large pike are caught.

There is no public access to the ponds and this also applies to a specially designated nature area, which has a breeding population of common tern. Also present on site are kingfisher, heron, plus tawny and little owl and sparrowhawk.

3. An obvious footpath sweeps right and ascends via steps onto the Leeds and Liverpool Canal. The link to the Bridgewater was cut towards the end of the 18th century with two economic benefits quickly appreciated by men with their eye on a fortune. Not only was a link to the Bridgewater an obvious advantage but also the vast deposits of coal in the Leigh area could be exported more cheaply by water.

4. Continue along the towpath towards Worsley and the Bridgewater until Twist Bridge is reached. Cross the bridge and turn left following the towpath on the opposite side. Ignore one bridge and at the next bridge cross and turn left.

5. Continue on this path but look out to the right. This is the former site of one of the largest collieries in Lancashire. Bickershaw operated until the closures following Nationalisation but miners had

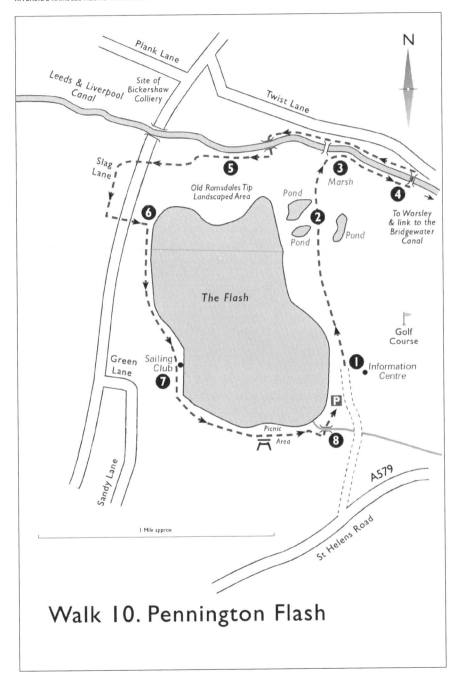

Walk 10. Pennington Flash

A view of the flash close to the Visitor Centre

been burrowing beneath what is now the Flash from the early 19th century. Mining reached a peak around the time of the First World War. Cross the evocatively named Slag Lane, turn left and then left again, crossing Slag Lane for the second time.

6. Approach the bank of Pennington Flash and prepare for a long period of observation. The site has been censused for many years by the Leigh Ornithological Society (01942 884 644). Numbers and populations of wildfowl and waders have increased recently, thanks to a cessation of unauthorised shooting.

7. Almost opposite Green Lane, the track passes a sailing club on the bank of the Flash. Ambitious landscaping of old coal spoil heaps, and associated railway tracks have produced a variety of habitats. Indigenous hardwoods including oak are now maturing well and, as the flora matures, the variety is increasing.

8. Keep following the footpath around the flash passing a picnic site on the left and crossing a bridge over a tributary of Hey Brook, which flows out of the flash. Turn left and return to the Information Centre.

Walk 11: Agden and Lymm

Directions: The route to Agden Bridge is via the M6 and the M56. Exit at Junction 7 and follow the A56 towards Warrington. After about three miles turn right onto the B5159. This passes under the Bridgewater Canal at Agden. It is possible to base this walk around Lymm, but those in search of a canal trek will prefer to start at Agden where there is some parking. At Lymm there are pay-and-display car parks. This would reduce the circular walk by 3 miles.

Public Transport: There is a regular bus service (37) linking Warrington with Altrincham. It passes close to Agden (alight at the junction of the A56 and the B5159). The bus also stops at Lymm.

Map Reference: OS Explorer 276 and 267 Grid Reference 715 866

Distance: 6½ miles

Time: 3½ hours

Lymm does not figure so much in tourists' handbooks these days, mainly because of the on-going problems with the Thelwall viaduct and the fact that the M6 is such a busy road. Here is the chance to escape for a slice of rural tranquillity in Lymm. The history of this area goes back before recorded time, for the rocks have revealed huge footprints of dinosaurs. Many of these fossils have been quarried from the rock and are displayed in the Manchester Museum.

Lymm must have been a delightful settlement until the 18th century when human engineering began to impact on the Mersey Valley. This walk passes along the Bridgewater Canal, along some of the old turnpike roads of the Georgian period, close to the Trans-Pennine trail (once a railway line at this point) and provides views of the Thelwall viaduct (see walk 19). Thus, every transport period is represented.

The Route

1. Firstly, explore Agden Wharf, which sells books and souvenirs as well as provisions for boaters. This ensures plenty of colour and activity. This is an ideal place to soak up more information about the Bridgewater and discover additional strolls in this area.

2. Follow the towpath keeping the canal on the left. In the summer,

Market cross and stocks, Lymm

this is the place to watch dragonflies and damselflies. Their continual presence proves that pollution levels are low. Anglers and boaters will each confirm these heartening facts. When strolling along canals I always carry a small collapsible net and a plastic margarine container. My most recent 'dip' produced dragonfly and caddis fly larvae; winter collections are important because these insects do not fly in the colder months, but spend their larval period in the mud of ponds, rivers and canals.

Warning: If you encourage children to 'canal stroll and dip' ensure that they are supervised and are aware of the dangers of water, however shallow it may seem. Always remember to examine your collection of aquatic creatures and then return them to the place from where you got them. This is conservation in action.

3. Continue along the canal and at this stage ignore the bridge over the A6144, which leads down into Lymm.

4. Continue to the next bridge, from which a minor road leads to Statham. A footpath from the village leads to the Manchester Ship Canal, crossing the Trans-Pennine trail and the old course of the

Mersey. This adds 2 miles or so but students of the river cannot afford to miss this area, which is quite literally a backwater.

5. Return to the canal towpath to Ditchfield's Bridge.

6. Cross the bridge and turn left. At the next road junction, turn right. Here, an area of water known as The Dingle is separated from Lymm Dam by the A56 road. All who love boats should explore the Dingle. This is a stream, which now leads down to the ship canal, but a pool area has been created and a steep little valley carries water beneath the road.

7. From the Dingle turn right and follow the footpath around Lymm Dam. This is unusual in the sense that some think that it is natural whilst others state that it stores the water needed to operate locks on the canal. The truth is that the Bridgewater over most of its length is a contour canal, following the geographical ups and downs, and it does not require locks. Actually, the truth is almost stranger than fiction because the dam was built by road builders during the days of the turnpikes.

A vitally important route between Manchester and Liverpool had to negotiate the very steep and often slippery Eagle Brow. The coaches had to turn sharply around the market cross (see stop 9) and then up to the church. On too many days, the road was not passable and so, in the 1850s, a decision was made. A ravine was dammed and a causeway built across it. This avoided the steep climb up to the church.

8. Follow the route around the dam, which looks as if it has been there for centuries. In some ways, this is a better winter walk because there are many wildfowl including the occasional rarity. The trees are also devoid of leaves and allow good views of the church, which also looks older than it actually is.

St Mary's church was extensively restored at the time that the dam was constructed. There is evidence, however, to show that there was a Christian focus in and around the area from Saxon times.

The church also has its share of legend. This concerns an old lady who visited the site every day. Each time she prayed she drank water from a spout fed by a spring. Then one day a hand emerged

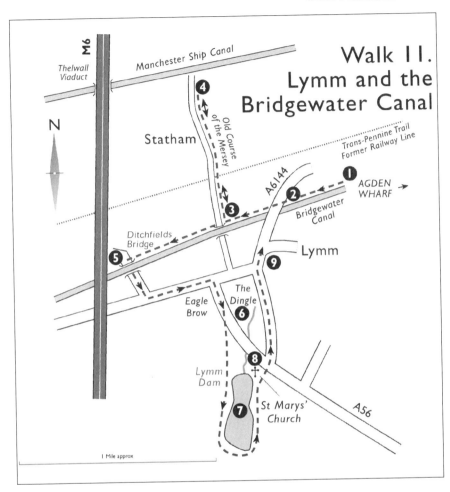

M6

Thelwall
Viaduct

Manchester Ship Canal

Walk 11.
Lymm and the
Bridgewater Canal

N

Statham

Old Course
of the Mersey

A6144

Trans-Pennine Trail
Former Railway Line

AGDEN →
WHARF

Bridgewater
Canal

Lymm

Ditchfields
Bridge

Eagle
Brow

The
Dingle

Lymm
Dam

St Marys'
Church

A56

1 Mile approx

from the spout and knocked away her water. This warned her that this was Holy Water and not for human consumption.

Until the Industrial Revolution, everyone realised that pure water was a blessing. For many years, the poor old Mersey was cursed but thankfully, things have now changed.

One tradition that has been at least partially restored to Lymm is the Rush Bearing ceremony. This relates to the time when churches had earthen floors. These were strewn with sweet smelling herbs and apart from the aroma the plants also served to keep the feet of

71

the worshippers warm. In medieval times, only the very rich had pews which had their initials carved on them.

The bulk of the parishioners were located in the centre of the nave. The infirm were allowed to lean on the wall – hence the origin of 'the weakest went to the wall'. All the able-bodied population gathered to collect rushes. The church welcomed the rush carts and in exchange provided 'free ale'.

9. From the church, bear right and then left across the A56 and into the centre of Lymm. Lymm should not be regarded as a mere suburb of Warrington but as a wealthy village made even wealthier by the coming of the Bridgewater Canal. After the canal, Lymm developed as an important centre for the production of fustian cloth. This is a combined fabric made up partly of cotton and partly of flax. The latter was important in the Warrington area as it was used in the production of sailcloth.

Look out for the magnificent set of stocks and the nearby market cross dating from the 17th century. Some think that the steps leading up to the cross may date from the 14th century and that they were carved directly into the underlying rock. There was a sensitive restoration in 1897 to celebrate Queen Victoria's Diamond Jubilee. It is safe to assume that they could hardly 'restore' the steps!

From Lymm return to the Bridgewater Canal and onwards to Agden.

Walk 12: The Bridgewater and Norton Priory

Directions: From the M56 exit at Junction 11. Follow the A56 towards Frodsham. At a point where the road crosses the canal, look out for a pub and Preston Brook. The Marina is always colourful with boats passing by or laid up for hire or repair.

Public Transport: Train station at Frodsham. Bus services from Frodsham, Runcorn, Chester and Warrington.

Map Reference: OS Explorer 266 & 275 Grid Reference 545 830

Distance: 5½ miles (7 miles if you follow all the footpaths around Norton Priory). The energetic may also like to take in a stroll to Daresbury.

Time: 3 to 4 hours depending upon how much you enjoy abbeys and churches.

If you were to compile a list of the North West's tourist attractions, I doubt if Runcorn would be mentioned even as an "also ran". However, two aspects of this walk ensure that the watercourses that make up the Mersey catchment, must be visited. These are Norton Priory and all that is left of the Runcorn branch of the Bridgewater Canal.

Norton Priory is a gem. In 1115, the Baron of Halton founded an Augustinian Priory, which was actually in Halton, but in 1134 the monks moved to a better site. The Priory became very rich and was still powerful at the time of its dissolution in 1536, on the orders of Henry VIII. In 1545, the buildings and estate were sold to Sir Richard Brooke and his descendants remained at Norton until 1921.

The Brookes eventually built two mansions on the site. The first was in Tudor times but a fine Georgian house later replaced this, which was a magnificent building reaching its peak around 1820. By 1970, most traces of these houses had long gone and the whole estate was an untidy mass of vegetation. Since 1970, archaeologists have unearthed many of the Priory treasures. Here is a museum, a shop and woodland trails – all splendidly maintained by a charitable trust.

Some original structures have been uncovered and the undercroft and passage of the monastery are in a splendid state of repair. These date from around 1200 and were used as storerooms. There is also a huge statue of St Christopher, which was carved in 1391. It is fitting that this statue of the patron saint of travellers should be at Norton, as it was a popular resting-place across the Mersey. There was no easy crossing before the days of bridges and tunnels (see walk 24).

The present-day Trust has maintained the statue theme by commissioning works for the gardens, which lead down to the canal. A stroll hereabouts is a real mix of the ancient and modern. There are stone coffins and the efficient drainage system of the old priory is largely intact. Here too is a bell cast from a mould made in the 12th century and found during the excavations. Among the modern artefacts is a life-sized statue of the Madonna and, in the middle of a small pond, is a statue of Coventina, the Celtic goddess of springs and wells.

A visit to Runcorn reveals the end of the Bridgewater Canal, which has been swamped by modern developments. The Runcorn branch has now been sealed at Waterloo Bridge but it originally descended via an impressive flight of ten locks, down into Runcorn Docks until it reached the Mersey. Into these docks there were connections to the Weaver Navigation and the Runcorn and Weston Canal. This entire complex became less important following the building of the Manches-

The old drainage system at the priory

ter Ship Canal in 1894. These locks were only filled in 1966; sadly, recent efforts to re-open them have not yet received funding.

The Route

1. Preston Brook Marina is close to where the A56 road crosses the Trent and Mersey. Close by to the south is the junction with the Bridgewater. The Trent and Mersey is well worth a walk in its own right but this route is along and around the Bridgewater.

2. Follow the towpath, keeping to the west of the towpath. Follow a well-maintained track towards the viaduct over the M56. The Preston Brook Marina is now on the opposite bank. The Bridgewater leads to Manchester (to the right) and Runcorn to the left. Follow the Runcorn Branch.

3. Cross the West Coast railway line and bear left away from the canal for a short distance. Look away to the left and see a rotunda-like building. Built of local sandstone this, the Norton Water Tower, provided a head of water to increase the pressure in local taps.

   Follow through a housing estate. Bear right and cross a bridge over the canal. Turn left onto the opposite bank. Look out over the Mersey towards Fiddlers Ferry Power Station (see walk 21). Look out to the right to see the Daresbury Atomic Research Station. Despite its worldwide reputation, the complex is threatened as national government is pressing for it to be relocated to the south of the country.

4. Approach Norton Town Bridge. To the left are St Mary's Church and Halton Castle. This area has a long and distinguished history with the few remnants of the castle dating back at least to Norman times and perhaps to the Iron Age, and certainly Saxon. The church, although it looks earlier, was designed by Sir Giles Gilbert Scott and consecrated in 1851.

5. This area is very interesting especially if you enjoy the architecture of canal bridges. After Norton Tower Bridge, you reach Norton Bridge (which is 72) and here is the chance to look down over the water as the towpath changes banks. Then come two more Norton bridges 73 and 74. At Greens Bridge (75) follow an obvious path to the gates of Norton Priory.

6. These days Norton Priory is set in 16 acres (6.5 hectares) of mixed

woodland through which runs a network of footpaths. Take time to enjoy the wildlife, which is fascinating. The Priory is open throughout the year but times vary, depending on the season; tel: 01928 569895. In April there are daffodils everywhere whilst between May and June there is a mass of bluebells.

There are now regular sightings of kingfishers in this area – a sure sign that the water quality is good enough to support fish. Birds are very intelligent. If there is not enough food for them to eat they do not die – they just go somewhere else. Look out for the 18th-century summerhouse, which functions as an excellent bird hide when the grounds are not too busy. Look out for redstarts during the summer.

7. Return from the Priory to the path and to Green's Bridge. Retrace the route towards Norton Town Bridge (71). Just after this ascend steps and then bear right down hill. After passing a small brook, go under an arch of the Warrington to Chester railway. Continue until a small bridge is reached.

8. Cross the bridge over Keckwith Brook and turn left. Follow marked signs to the right over another stream and then beneath yet another railway line – this time the West Coast route. This part of the walk really is a contrast between transport and industry on one hand and rural tranquillity on the other. There is much here that a famous local lad would still recognise.

An island farm, 'mid seas of corn
Swayed by the wandering breath of morn
This happy spot where I was born

– so wrote the Revd Charles Dodgson, Christened at All Saints church at nearby Daresbury in 1832, he is better known as Lewis Carroll. A stained glass window in the church shows characters from *Alice in Wonderland*. Follow a steep track and cross a field leading to steps back onto the canal.

9. Turn right. Pass Red Brow, which leads up to Daresbury. If you wish to add three miles to the journey, you could visit the *Alice* church. Then continue on meeting the junction with the Trent and Mersey Canal.

Cross a footbridge over the Runcorn branch of the Bridgewater, under the motorway viaduct and back to Preston Brook.

Walk 12. Bridgewater Canal, Preston Brook and Norton Priory

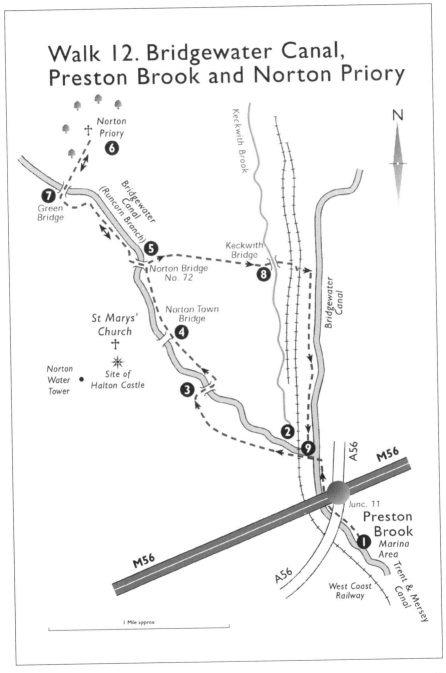

Norton Priory

Keckwith Brook

N

Bridgewater Canal (Runcorn Branch)

Green Bridge

Keckwith Bridge

Norton Bridge No. 72

St Marys' Church

Norton Town Bridge

Norton Water Tower

Site of Halton Castle

Bridgewater Canal

A56

M56

Junc. 11

Preston Brook

Marina Area

M56

A56

West Coast Railway

Trent & Mersey Canal

I Mile approx

SECTION 5: THE IRWELL

No river has been so consistently maligned as the Irwell, unless it is its tributaries of Roch, Croal, Irk and Medlock! Music Hall comedians joked that if you fell into it, you dissolved before you drowned!

There are two possible derivations of the name. It could be *Ere-well* meaning 'white spring' or *Irr-well* meaning 'dark river' due to the peaty soil at its source. This is between Burnley and Bacup from where the Irwell tumbles through the towns of Rawtenstall and Ramsbottom.

The catchment has had more of its share of man-made problems. What was a major salmon river and the haunt of otters became a stinking open sewer. Karl Marx and Frederick Engles stood at the windows of Chetham Library, looked down at the Irwell and penned the Communist Manifesto – The Dark River was not so much dark as pitch black.

On the summit of Holcombe Hill there is a tower erected in memory of Sir Robert Peel. It was built by public subscription in 1851 to celebrate the man whose fortune was generated by 'king cotton'. He entered politics, and founded the first police force in the 1820s. First they were called Peelers and then Bobbies. He was Prime Minister in the 1840s.

The original East Lancashire railway line terminated at Bury (see walk 13) by which point the Irwell merges with the Croal, which flows through Bolton. Until very recently the Croal was heavily polluted but it is now regarded as a major focus for walkers.

Reservoirs at Entwistle, Wayoh and Jumbles (See walk 14) have, thanks to the efforts of United Utilities, provided circular walks. Other industrial sites, especially at Moses Gate (see walk 15), which was once a massive chemical and papermaking complex, is now a delightful stroll, based upon a Visitor Centre with resident wardens.

Another major tributary is the Roch. Rochdale was settled in the Bronze Age and later had an important Roman road. Part of this is still seen over Blackstone Edge: proof that the Mersey catchment was an important trade and military route. There is no space here to write up a walk along the Roch. The Medlock, however, has one particularly bright spot, which has to be explored. This is Daisy Nook (see walk 16).

The construction of the Manchester Ship Canal in the 1890s disturbed this river valley route because the Irwell now merges with this cut. Formerly it flowed straight into the Mersey. The Irwell split the city of Manchester on one bank from the initially more important city of Salford on the other. On the Salford Bank still stands the ancient half-timbered Ordsall Hall (see walk 5).

Walk 13: Ramsbottom to Rawtenstall via the East Lancashire Steam Railway

Directions: The East Lancashire Railway (0161 764 7790) is signed from the M65 motorway and Rawtenstall station is at the intersection of the A681 and A682. There is plenty of parking by the side of the station. There is also parking at Ramsbottom station, which is close to the A56 and well signed. This linear walk can therefore be enjoyed in either direction.

Distance: A linear 5 miles (8 miles with diversions to Helmshore Textile Museum and Buckden Woods).

Time: Allow at least three hours

Map reference:OS Explorer 287 **Rawtenstall** – Grid Reference 815 233 **Ramsbottom** – Grid Reference 792 172

Public Transport: There are regular bus services to both Ramsbottom and Rawtenstall. Throughout the summer and on winter weekends East Lancashire Railway runs from Bury mainline station. Transport information from Rawtenstall Tourist Information Centre on 01706 226596.

This walk is part of the Irwell Way, which runs from Bacup to Manchester. This linear stroll encompasses a major chapter in the history of the cotton industry and is also a place to re-live the heady days of steam. The line opened in 1846 and, following the cuts, it closed for passengers in 1972 but the last freight train ran until 1980. Following a period of intense controversy, the line was saved. In 1987, there was a link between Bury and Ramsbottom and in 1991 it was extended to Rawtenstall. By 2005 it is hoped that the line will have been extended from Bury to Heywood and hopefully beyond to the main rail network.

The Walk

1. At Ramsbottom Station look up to see the Robert Peel Monument high on Holcombe Hill. There is also a Dickensian connection here because the novelist came to visit the Grant brothers. The two Scots made their fortune from Lancashire cotton but were very generous to their workers. Dickens used them as a model for his Cheeryble brothers in *Nicholas Nickleby*. The Grant's Arms celebrates the

79

The weir at Ramsbottom

brothers and offers good food, as does the appropriately named Railway Arms opposite the station. Telephone numbers – Grant's Arms 01706 823354; Railway Hotel 01706 821484.

2. Turn right out of the station to the level crossing. Cross the road and turn right. Look over the River Irwell on the left. The river is not polluted these days and the weir looks very attractive. This wide mini waterfall once accelerated the current to provide water for a mill, which now produces paper. Turn left and continue straight ahead following the riverside path. On the opposite bank of the Irwell is a small park with picnic tables.

3. Cross a stream and follow the obvious footpath alongside a stone wall. This reaches the A676 near Stubbins. Cross this and continue straight ahead which keeps the Irwell on the left. Pass a recreation ground and turn right onto a footpath.

4. Pass one of the many sculptures along the Irwell Way and follow a path that passes close to the railway but this is protected only by a stone wall. This area is much loved by railway enthusiasts because the engines have to negotiate a steep gradient and this means slow progress, lots of extra steam and spectacular photographic opportunities. Pass through a subway and follow the riverbank to a road. Turn left over a bridge over the Irwell and then sharp right along the opposite bank of the river.

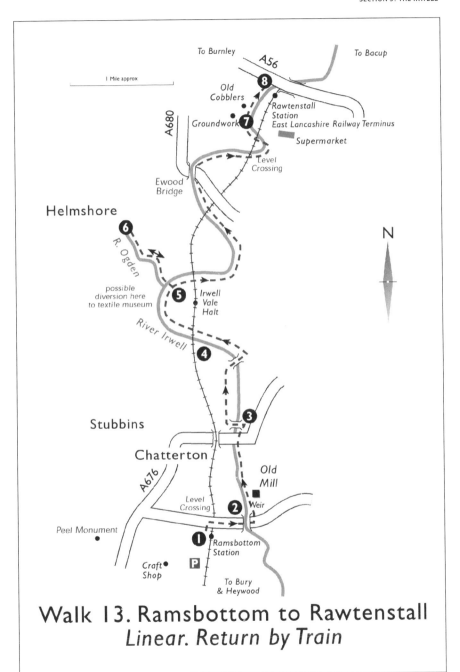

Walk 13. Ramsbottom to Rawtenstall
Linear. Return by Train

5. Irwell Vale, where the river Ogden meets the Irwell, is one of Lancashire's hidden secrets. In the early days of the Industrial Revolution, the watercourses powered the industries of villages of Lumb, Chatterton and Strongstry. As handloom weaving gave way to machines there was industrial strife. In 1820, Luddites rioted at Chatterton in the Plug Riots, when they removed the plugs from boilers, with the result that the army was brought in. Nine workers were killed and many more were injured.

Two worthwhile diversions adding around two miles

Each of these diversions is well signed from Irwell Vale, which has been designated a conservation area. For those who only wish to explore this area, there is a small station here.

Just to the west of Strongstry is Buckden Woods (meaning a place of the deer). Here are 435 acres (176 hectares) of wonderful woodland, which has been looked after by the National Trust since 1943. This is of great interest to naturalists whilst historians should not miss a stroll to Helmshore Textile Museum (01706 226459). This is one of the best of its type in the world and has a working water wheel. Here too are examples of early textile machinery including mules and water frames. There are working spinning and weaving machines operated by people who actually worked in the industry.

6. Return to Irwell Vale and turn right at the notice board indicating the village centre. Just before the railway subway, turn left at a finger post. Keep the railway to the right and, just before the Irwell, cross the railway (take care) and then keep the river on the left. This is a winding track and you have to cross the railway again.

Continue along the river to a sports ground and then to the B6527 at Ewood Bridge. Cross the road and continue to follow the path with the Irwell on the left.

7. The footpath passes beneath the A682 and along the riverbank to an Industrial Unit. Keep to the right of this complex and continue to Townsend Fold level crossing. Then turn left away from the railway, then cross the Irwell for the last time.

Turn right alongside the river to Rossendale Groundwork Trust, which has its headquarters in a restored cotton mill, complete with an isolated chimney. In the early days, chimneys were well named as *smoke pokes*. There is good parking here and nearby is the Old Cobblers (01706 211116) which is a pleasant pub overlooking the Irwell and the railway and with its own good car park.

Ramsbottom Station

8. Follow the obvious track through the small countryside park and pass more of the sculptures, a feature of the Irwell Way. After passing through a stone archway, cross the railway at the level crossing and then turn right into Rawtenstall Station. Return by steam train. There is also a good bus service on the route between Burnley and Bolton and from the X43 Burnley to Manchester.

Things to see at Rawtenstall from the station

- Ski Rossendale, a dry slope, is within strolling distance of the station and is well signed.

- So is the Whittaker Museum, set in delightful gardens, whilst within are reminders of old transport routes and of the cotton industry.

- Rossendale and the Upper Irwell made their fortune from the production of footwear and especially slippers. The Lambert Howarth Museum of footwear is advertised at the station.

- The only Temperance bar left in Britain is in Rawtenstall and this is the place to enjoy a pint of sarsaparilla. This is Fitzpatrick's Herbal Health (01706 211152). This is worth a visit because of the old copper hot water dispenser that was removed from the Empress Ballroom in Burnley.

Walk 14: The Croal Irwell – Jumbles Reservoir and Turton Tower

Directions: Jumbles Information Centre situated at Waterfold is reached from the A676 on Bradshaw Road, which links Ramsbottom to Bolton. Jumbles reservoir is signed to the right. Free parking by the Information Centre; tel: 01204 853360.

Public Transport: There are bus stops along the A676 but this obviously involves more walking. Ramblers with no car never worry about this sort of thing and the walk from the A676 to the Information Centre is less than one mile.

There is a station at Bromley Cross, which is on the main line between Bolton and Blackburn. There is at least an hourly service. This circular route can be started from Ouzel Nest close to point 3.

Map Reference: OS Explorer 287 Grid Reference 735 146. OS Sheet SD61/71

Distance: 4 miles

Time: Allow 3 hours to explore the wildlife as well as Turton Tower and its environs.

Jumbles reservoir looks as if it has been there for centuries. Wildfowl mingle happily among the colourful craft operated by the Civil Service Sailing Club.

It was, however, only opened in 1971 and constructed as a compensation reservoir. Its function was not to provide drinking water but to serve as a reserve supply, should water levels fall in the catchment. The dammed flow from Bradshaw Brook now feeds four million gallons per day into the Croal-Irwell system. The area of the reservoir is around 50 acres (20 hectares).

Much of the cotton history of the Bolton area is now submerged beneath the Jumbles, but the Information Centre has a little museum. This deals with the industrial history that evolved around Bradshaw Brook. Here there were watermills, farms and little cottages until the onset of the Industrial Revolution.

As early as 1830, Bolton's ambitious manufacturers were demanding more and more water for their mills and associated housing.

By 1831 a reservoir had been built in the Turton/Entwistle area and in 1876 another was constructed at Wayoh. In line with the enlightened environmental policy of the water companies United Utilities have recently produced walking trails around each of these reservoirs.

This present walk, so full of fascinating reminders of an industrial past and so rich in natural history, has an additional attraction – an impressive old hall at Turton. Turton is chronicled at least to 1212 and, at that time, ancient Saxon lands had been usurped by Roger Fitz-Robert and Henry the Duke of Lancaster. By 1420 the extensive manor was owned by the Orrel family and it was they who developed the Tower as their power base. It was constructed around a medieval pele tower, built as a defence against the invading Scots. By the late 16th century it was a half-timbered substantial manor house with an associated farm. It is still set in beautiful grounds. Turton Tower is now a museum containing a collection of old weapons, suits of armour, period furniture and incorporates a shop and a cosy little tearoom; tel: 01204 852203.

Turton Tower

The Route

1. From the car park follow the obvious footpath and descend along the side of the reservoir embankment.

2. Look closely at the area at a bridge over a weir feeding compensation water from the reservoir. This bubbles oxygen into the water thus providing food for such aquatic creatures as stonefly and mayfly. These, and other creatures, provide food for the resident dipper and grey wagtail.

   A look downstream to Bradshaw Brook will reveal some of the glorious scenery, which must have graced this area before industry took a heavy hand. Nature, however, is the great healer and there are now good populations of fish including brown trout. This attracts kingfisher, heron and sadly the occasional mink.

3. At the end of the bridge cross a stile and bear slightly left towards the black and white mock Tudor Ouzel Nest Field Cottage. Veer to the right to meet Grange Road, cross a stile and turn right. Along Grange Road a sign indicates Ouzel Nest car park. The word 'ouzel' was once used instead of 'thrush' and both song- and mistle-thrushes breed in the area.

4. Approach Grange Farm, with its stables. Pass through gates (take care to close them behind you) and then between an avenue of trees dominated by horse chestnut and lime.

5. Continue along the obvious track and reach the Civil Service Sailing Club on the right. The area of Horrobin Fold, once almost derelict, has been restored and the old cottages are a joy to behold.

   Cross the bridge over Hazelhurst Brook, which is a tributary of Bradshaw Brook. Turn left up and along Horrobin Lane.

6. Horrobin Lane these days seems to be going nowhere but was once the access road to the complex of Horrobin mills. These now lie beneath the waters of Jumbles reservoir.

7. Follow the signs for Turton Tower. A walk in the grounds leads to a bridge over the railway line which links Blackburn and Darwen to Bolton. This was built between 1845 and 1848. At this time, the Tower belonged to the Kay family who objected to their views being disrupted. The compromise was to ensure that the bridges over the line resembled castles and these are still with us to this

Walk 14. Jumbles Reservoir and Turton Tower

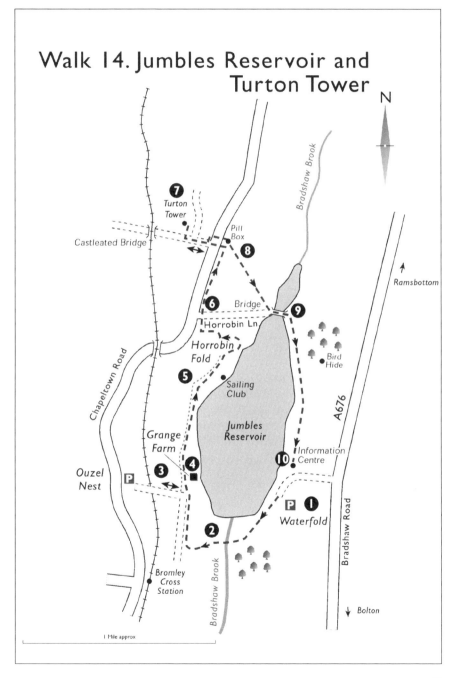

N

Bradshaw Brook

7 Turton Tower

Pill Box

Castleated Bridge

8

Ramsbottom

6 Bridge **9**

Horrobin Ln

Horrobin Fold

Chapeltown Road

Bird Hide

5

Sailing Club

A676

Jumbles Reservoir

Grange Farm

3 **4**

Information Centre

10

Ouzel Nest

P

P **1**

Waterfold

Bradshaw Road

2

Bromley Cross Station

Bradshaw Brook

Bolton

1 Mile approx

day. The walk leading up to bridge attracts naturalists particularly in spring when the flowers are in full bloom especially the blue-bells, whilst the autumn tree colours and fungi are a treat. The woodlands in the area provide breeding habitat for many birds including the blackcap.

8. Return from Turton Tower via Chapeltown Road and approach the site of a Second World War pillbox. Usually regarded as concrete monstrosities but some (if not all) of these structures should be retained as part of our history. Cross the road and look for a stile. Cross this and continue to a footbridge over a narrowed area of Jumbles reservoir.

9. Turn right and follow a well-marked trail through a wooded area eventually leading to a bird hide. In winter this affords excellent views of wildfowl. Species here include pochard, goldeneye, goosander, tufted duck, mute swan and, in winter, the occasional herd of wintering whooper swans. All this proves that nature soon adapts to environmental changes, providing that pollution levels are low.

10. The Information Centre museum should be enjoyed at the end of the walk once the geographical setting is set in context.

The tenants of Bradshaw Hall once owned Bradshaw Brook. By the 17th century, wool and linen mills were operating and later cotton and especially bleach works were established. Paper mills were all close by and there was also some coal mining. Many artefacts associated with these industries are on display in the Centre. Also here is an impressive natural history exhibition.

Jumbles has good toilet facilities and there are picnic tables carefully sited to combine good views and sheltered crannies. This is why Jumbles is a good choice for a winter ramble.

It is only when following small tributaries such as Bradshaw Brook that the extensive catchment of the Mersey can be appreciated. Each of these streams once carried a load of pollutants, which eventually reached the Mersey estuary via the Croal and the Irwell.

SECTION 5: THE IRWELL

Walk 15: Moses Gate – Three Waters and Two Parks

Directions: From the M61 turn off at Junction 3. Follow the A666 through Kearsley and Farnworth. Moses Gate Country Park is signed off the A666 and reached along Hall Lane where there is plenty of free parking.

Public Transport: There are regular rail services to Farnworth. This is close to Moses Gate. The next station along the line from Bolton towards Salford is at Kearsley. This is within strolling distance of Clifton Country Park, which is about half way along this circular route.

Map Reference: OS Explorer 276 & 277 Grid Reference 740 075

Distance: 6½ miles

Time: Allow 3½ hours

In the 1970s a list was compiled of the most polluted rivers in Europe. The Mersey merited a dishonourable mention as did the Croal and the Irwell.

This walk, starting from Moses Gate, is set at the confluence of the Croal with the Irwell. It is not a surprise to find that, at one time, the area was so heavily polluted that nothing could live there. At times, any bird that ventured into the river could literally walk on the slime of pollution, which smothered the surface. The modern miracle of this walk follows three watercourses. These are the Manchester, Bury and Bolton Canal, the Croal and the Irwell – each of which is now rich in wildlife.

Moses Gate Country Park is composed of 750 acres (300 hectares) of what has been described as *Urban Countryside*. It is looked after by an efficient Warden Service (01204 571561). The team is located in what is left of Rock Hall. This was built in 1807 by the Crompton family but they did not live in it themselves. They built the much larger Vale House not far from Rock Hall, but this has long since been demolished and has disappeared.

Rock Hall's Information Centre traces the history of the Croal-Irwell Valley back to the Ice Ages. The rivers were much in demand as the Industrial Revolution gathered pace. Workers poured in to seek employment in coalmines, bleach works, cotton mills, chemical works and paper mills. By the 1830s the river systems were so polluted that reservoirs had to be built to provide fresh water. These ponds are very much part of the attractions now enjoyed on this walk.

The Route

1. Start at the reservoir areas (known as lodges) close to the car park. The Crompton family made most of their vast fortune from the production of paper. This industry could not function without copious volumes of very clean water. In recent years more than 130 species of bird have been recorded around these ponds and little grebes breed in the area. From the Visitor Centre, bear right to the River Croal.

2. The River Croal around the weir is now a major location for bird-watchers. Fish are present on the whole stretch from the centre of Bolton to the confluence with the Irwell. This encourages the king-fisher, which is frequently seen, along with grey wagtail and the dipper – both of which are resident. There are also some sightings of the summer-visiting common sandpiper.

3. Bear right following the meander of the River Croal and then cross over the river via a bridge. The path bears right through an area known as Canal Wood.

    In the 1970s, lots of sensible planting went on with native species such as alder, birch, willow and poplar being the initial choices. The Red Rose Forest team is now skilfully managing this area, which is one cog in a mighty Community Forest project for Greater Manchester.

    The area around the Croal is constantly changing for the better. The 1970s plantings have been thinned to make room for oak and hazel – these species help the return of flowers and a varied assortment of animals.

4. Keep bearing right and follow the towpath of the Manchester, Bolton and Bury Canal. Keep the canal on the left and pass through an area known as Red Rocks. Those who are interested in the geology of the Mersey Valley will note a geological fault, which pushed several coal seams closer to the surface. In consequence, this meant that coal mining became important in the area. The dominant rock

Walk 15. Moses Gate and the Croal-Irwell

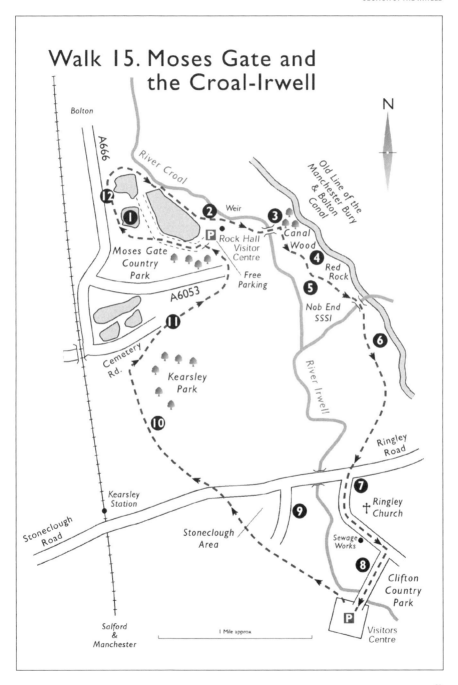

N

Bolton

A666

River Croal

Old Line of the Manchester & Bury Bolton Canal

Weir

Canal Wood

Rock Hall Visitor Centre

Moses Gate Country Park

Red Rock

Free Parking

A6053

Nob End SSSI

Cemetery Rd.

Kearsley Park

River Irwell

Ringley Road

Kearsley Station

Ringley Church

Stoneclough Road

Stoneclough Area

Sewage Works

Clifton Country Park

Salford & Manchester

I Mile approx

Visitors Centre

in the area is a red sandstone known as Nob End sandstone and which is unique to this area.

5. Follow the obvious footpath through Nob End. Despite a history of intense industrial development this site is now so well endowed with natural history that it has been declared a Site of Special Scientific Interest (SSSI).

By the 1790s, Nob End had a large sulphuric acid factory and was followed in 1884 by a washing soda plant. Waste material contaminated the land although this has proved to be something of a blessing in disguise. The alkaline deposits have produced an ideal habitat for some rare plants, especially orchids; hence the SSSI designation.

6. Continue along a path with the old line of the Manchester, Bury and Bolton Canal on the left. This was opened as early as 1796 and built specifically to provide transport of materials sited along the Croal-Irwell valley. Look out for an old dry dock and, to the left, a set of six locks at Prestolee. A serious attempt is being made to restore at least part of the disused canal, which deserves to become a tourist attraction. There are old packhorse bridges, showing that this area is still criss-crossed with ancient tracks.

7. Continue into the village of Ringley, which underlines these old associations. Near to the church seek out a set of 17th-century stocks and a packhorse bridge dating from 1677. It was along these routes that the handloom weavers carried their woollen cloth to the markets in Bury or Manchester. Each roll of cloth was sold by the piece and thus, we have the origin of the word 'piecework'.

8. From the church and Fold Road follow a track past a sewage works on the left and enter Clifton Country Park. Clifton Bridge is an interesting span although it was only built in 1992. It crosses the Irwell and provides a link to Ringley. It also links the Boroughs of old Salford with Bolton.

Clifton Lake has settled so well into the landscape that it is difficult to believe that it was only dug in the 1960s during the extraction of gravel to build the M62 motorway (see also walk 18).

A few minutes' stroll leads to the Visitor Centre, from which paths radiate through grassland, woodland and wetland areas. The route around the park is wheelchair friendly.

Decision Time

Those who use public transport may wish to conclude their walk here and return home via Kearsley station. Those with their own transport will find the rest of this walk just as fascinating as the inward half.

Although quite rare, redwings may be seen along the Croal-Irwell catchment in some winters

9. Out of Clifton Country Park, sweep to the right, passing the Stoneclough Trading Estate and crossing Stoneclough Road. The railway is to the left. Continue into Kearsley Park.

10. Kearsley Park is a pleasant area with the railway on the left and the ever-cleaner Irwell on the right. For many centuries, migrating birds have used rivers as a final navigation. Fieldfares are often seen feeding in grassland and wooded areas and this Scandinavian-based species is often joined by redwings. The migration pattern of the redwing is more difficult to comprehend as they travel at night. In some winters waxwings are recorded throughout the Mersey Valley. The species normally winters in the Scandinavian conifer forests. Should this crop fail (which it does every ten years or so) then waxwings irrupt into Britain and feed on berries such as hawthorn. The name derives from the patch of red on its wings which looks like a dab of sealing wax once used to seal letters and parcels before the days of glue and adhesive tape.

11. Pass the confluence of the Irwell and the Croal and follow the latter keeping the river on the right. Pass Darley Park and the cemetery on the left and bear left into Moses Gate Country Park.

12. Take time to follow the boardwalk routes around the lodges. There are plenty of seats on which to picnic and enjoy bird watching. You may have to share your food with grey squirrels.

Walk 16: The Medlock and Daisy Nook

Directions: Situated along Newmarket Road, just off the A627 between Oldham and Ashton. The recent extension to the M60 motorway has caused some disruption but this has now settled down. Junctions 22 or 23 off the M60 are within easy driving distance of Daisy Nook Country Park. Parking is free and there is a pleasant café on site. Details available from Park Bridge Country Park: 0161 330 9613.

Public Transport: From Ashton and Oldham railway stations there are bus routes passing Daisy Nook Country Park. Look for numbers 382, 232 or 233 or ring 0161 228 7811.

Map Reference: OS Explorer 277 Grid Reference 920 010

Distance: 4 miles

Time: 1½ to 2 hours but allow extra time to enjoy the ever-richer wildlife on offer.

The River Medlock rises close to Bishop Park to the north-east of Oldham and flows between Oldham and Ashton – and then into one of the most urban areas of Manchester. After some ten miles from its source the Medlock feeds into the Irwell.

There were very few bright spots as the Medlock became both used and abused by industries especially those associated with coal and cotton. Daisy Nook was one of few pleasant places along the Medlock Valley and became popular with the Victorians especially during the Easter Fair. This tradition continues to the present day.

As pollution loads were reduced Daisy Nook was set up as a Country Park in 1974 following local government reorganisation. Many factors revitalised the Medlock Valley, including the closure of many textile operations, which is a mixed blessing in terms of employment.

Large sums of money have been invested by United Utilities to modernise sewage works and all industries now have a keen eye on their environmental impact. The watchdog of these pollution loads was the National Rivers' Authority, which has now been renamed the Environment Agency. Their role in improving the environment has to be regarded as crucial because they can compel companies to control their pollutants, which could find their way into watercourses.

Waterhouses aqueduct, with the River Medlock below

As part of the Daisy Nook scheme a warden service was initiated, trees were planted and the watercourses so improved that school children began to enjoy their lessons in ecology.

Within the Medlock Valley these days there are quiet parks and areas for anglers, horse riders, walkers, naturalists, boaters and those who just want to stop and stare at the stunning views.

The Route

1. Begin at the Visitors' Centre. Some time should be spent in obtaining the informative leaflets, which show that orienteering, model boat sailing, bridleways and strolls along nature trails are becoming increasingly popular. If all these paths are explored it could add a mile or two to this route but it is well worth it.

2. From the Visitors' Centre bear right and follow the path keeping Oak Hill to the left. Turn left over the Waterhouses Aqueduct, which once carried the Hollinwood Canal over the Medlock. The word Hollinwood appears throughout Britain – explained by the fact that the old word for Holly was Hollin. From the substantial aqueduct, turn left and follow the bank of the Medlock.

3. Approach Stannybrook Road and turn right along this. Down to the left is the site of the Easter Fair.

4. Continue along Stannybrook Road to the Crime View Inn and the lake, which gives the hostelry its name. Crime Lake sounds like a place that the police should keep a wary eye on but walkers can rest easy because **Crime** is only an old local word meaning a meadow.

How ancient is Crime Lake? The answer is not very old and it can be regarded as an *accidental* lake. It was created when a bank of the canal collapsed and flooded the area. As the ground contains a lot of clay the floodwater was retained and the Lake has given local folk a lot of pleasure for almost 200 years!

5. After enjoying the natural history around Crime Lake or partaking of a pie and a pint or a coffee at the Inn turn right and cross a small aqueduct over the Hollinwood Canal. After the aqueduct turn left and keep the canal on the left.

Looking at the complex canal routes with a modern eye would seem to suggest a lack of design. What should not be forgotten is that there used to be many small coalmines, and these were only profitable if transport to Manchester and the surrounding area was easy and cheap. The canals were cut to access these mines and other industries.

The Ashton-under-Lyne Canal Act was passed in 1792 and allowed a construction of a 6½-mile cut from the Piccadilly area of Manchester from which other existing canals could be linked. From Piccadilly the canal was cut to Dukinfield, where there were many pits. The original idea was that it would operate as an independent canal but it was soon linked with the Huddersfield Narrow and the Lower Peak Forest Canals.

In the context of this walk two other linking canals are of interest. The Hollinwood Branch opened in 1796 and, the following year, the Fairbottom section came on line. Continue along the Hollinwood Branch to reach one of the most interesting stops on this walk.

6. At the Waterhouses Junction time should be taken to explore the canal geography. To the right the Hollinwood Canal main line leads off via a pair of locks called a *staircase* and then down into an

Walk 16. Daisy Nook on the Medlock

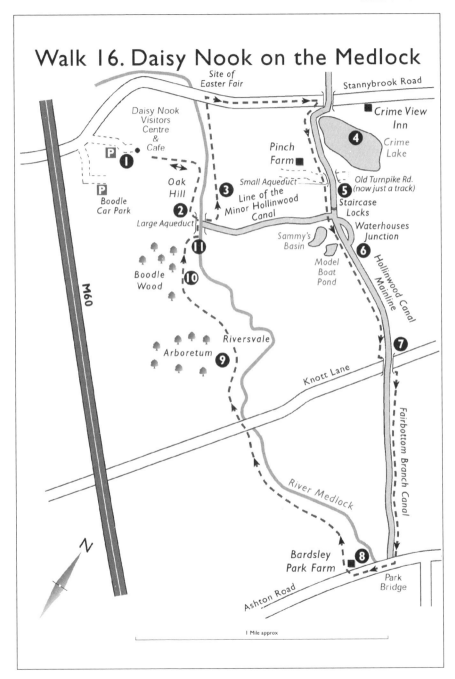

Site of
Easter Fair

Stannybrook Road

Daisy Nook
Visitors
Centre
&
Cafe

Crime View
Inn

Crime
Lake

Pinch
Farm

Old Turnpike Rd.
(now just a track)

Oak
Hill

Small Aqueduct

Line of the
Minor Hollinwood
Canal

Boodle
Car Park

Staircase
Locks

Large Aqueduct

Waterhouses
Junction

Sammy's
Basin

Boodle
Wood

Model
Boat
Pond

M60

Riversvale

Arboretum

Knott Lane

River Medlock

Bardsley
Park Farm

Park
Bridge

Ashton Road

Hollinwood Canal Mainline

Fairbottom Branch Canal

1 Mile approx

97

old pound known as Sammy's Basin. This is popular with anglers and so is a stretch of the old canal now known as the Model Boat Pond. Explore this area but then return to Waterhouses Junction and turn right. The route now keeps the Fairbottom Branch Canal on the left.

7. Continue to the bridge over Knott Lane. Cross the canal and turn sharp right. Then follow the towpath keeping the canal on the right. This area is popular with anglers.

8. Approach the A627 (Ashton Road) and turn right along this to Bardsley Car Park. Some prefer to use this area as the base for the circular stroll especially at busy periods.

9. At this point the route follows the meander of the River Medlock. Keep the river to the right, cross Knott Lane and continue to the arboretum. This is an ideal place to learn how to identify trees and this is one of many reasons why this walk should be enjoyed at all seasons. It enables winter buds, spring blossoms, autumn fruits and falling leaves to be identified.

10. Continue towards and into Boodle Wood. This gives the chance to look at the trees to test how well the information provided in the arboretum has been assimilated.

11. From Boodle Wood the path swings right and then left before crossing the Waterhouses Aqueduct for the second time. Return to the Visitors' Centre.

SECTION 6: THE MERSEY VALLEY

This stretch between Stockport and Widnes is a wonderful example of the resilience of the Mersey and its tributaries, some of which are still not thought to relate to the main river at all. Take the Micker Brook, for example, which joins the Mersey at Cheadle. Visitors around this confluence should cast their eyes upstream and think history. This little stream is confusing because it keeps changing its name. Micker Brook becomes Ladybrook, close to the magnificent Bramall Hall. Then it becomes Norbury Brook and, close to its source, it is known as Bollinghurst Brook. This flows close to the magnificent old house at Lyme Park.

Bramall Hall is described in walk 17, but space precludes a similar stroll around Lyme Park. Those who wish to enjoy this walk can contact Lyme Park Rangers' Office on 01663 762023.

Sometimes modern developments can bestow ecological advantages on an area and the present M60 has certainly done this. Gravel extraction during construction has led to the development of Sale Water Park (see walk 18) and Chorlton Water Park, yet another walk which is not described here due to lack of space. Canal construction in the Mersey Valley has also bestowed some advantages. These can be seen in walks 19, 20 and 21.

Walk 17: The Mersey Valley and Bramall Hall

Directions: Care is needed because Bramall Hall (0161 485 4681) is in the village of Bramhall and not in Stockport. From the M60 exit at Junction 21 and follow the A5102 to Bramhall. There are some (but not enough) brown signs indicating the hall. Take care to follow Carrwood Road and look for the Bramall Hall sign. Take the first and smallest of the two pay-and-display car parks.

The village of Bramhall is spelt with an 'h' but Bramall Hall omits the 'h'. This leads to some confusion but it has been the case for centuries.

Map Reference: OS Explorer 268 & OL1 Grid Reference 891 865

Public Transport: There are railway stations at Bramhall and Cheadle Hulme. There is a regular bus route from Stockport numbers 377 and 378.

Distance: 3½ miles (including the woodland diversions)

Time: Allow 3-4 hours including a tour of the hall.

B efore the Norman Conquest Bramall was made up of two separate manors owned by the Saxon lords Brun and Hacun. Around 1070, after brutally snuffing out Saxon unrest, William the Conqueror gave both manors to one of his followers – Hamon de Masai who was also made the first Baron Dunham Massey (see walk 8).

For the next 800 years only three families owned the manor of Bramall. These were the Masseys, the de Bromales who ran out of male heirs in the late 14th century, and then the Davenports – who were in residence for five centuries. It is this continuity of ownership, which accounts for the glory of this black and white masterpiece, sections of which date back to the 14th century. Of special note are the great hall and the Oriel window overlooking the courtyard.

This window is supported by a piece of solid timber called a *corbel*. The carving on this shows an angel holding a shield on which is depicted the de Bromale Coat of Arms. Clearly this is Christian but a close look at a male head shows sprays of oak leaves emerging from his mouth. This clearly depicts the *Green Man*, which is Celtic in origin.

Bramall Hall

The green man was at the centre of spring fertility celebrations, which were suppressed by Christian teachings eager to mourn the Crucifixion over Easter. This window, however, shows that even in the 14th and 15th centuries, the old religion was not dead!

It is easy to see why, in Celtic times, people worshipped wildlife and water. The Mersey and its tributaries were full of fish and the woodland abounded with game.

The Route

1. Start at the smaller of the two car parks. Bear left and descend into an extensive area of mature woodland. According to the season this is the place to hear bird song, identify flowers, watch grey squirrels on the hunt for fruit or appreciate the wonderful colours of the fungi. Follow the path that sweeps gently to the right and pass a pond on the left.

2. At the pond bear right close to the picnic tables. Then turn left and pass between two ponds.

3. At the obvious wooden footbridge cross the river and turn sharp right. Ensure that you keep to the path closest to the Ladybrook,

Walk 17. Bramall Hall

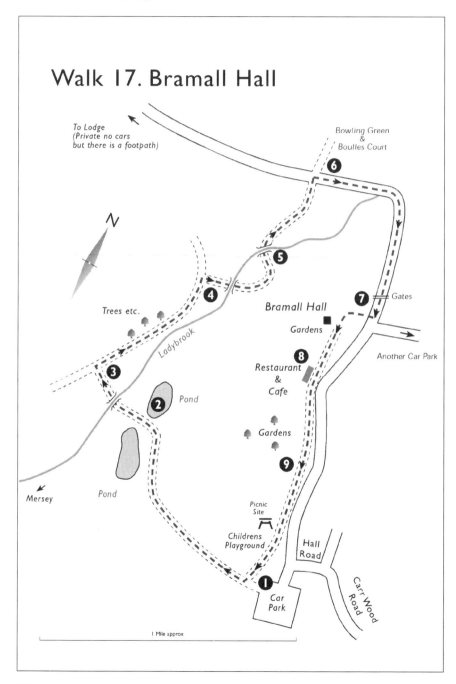

To Lodge
(Private no cars
but there is a footpath)

Bowling Green
&
Boulles Court

6

N

5

4

Gates

7

Trees etc.

Bramall Hall

Gardens

Ladybrook

Another Car Park

3

8

Restaurant
&
Cafe

2 Pond

Gardens

9

Mersey

Pond

Picnic
Site

Childrens
Playground

Hall
Road

1

Car
Park

Carr Wood Road

1 Mile approx

which is on the right. You are now on part of the Ladybrook Valley Interest Trail. Copies of this are on sale in the Hall shop.

4. Approach an area of substantial fencing leading onto a bridge. Turn right across this bridge but you may prefer to explore the woodland path for a while before returning to the bridge. This is the place to enjoy the variety of fauna and flora. Look out for greater spotted and green woodpecker as well as nuthatch, treecreeper and jay.

Return to the bridge and turn left. Look out to the right to view Bramall Hall seen at its best on the rising ground.

5. Bear left along a narrow metalled track. Cross the river again via a stone castellated bridge. After the bridge the path divides. Take the right fork. Note that the left fork leads to the lodge, which is *not open to the public.*

6. Ascend a gentle slope and approach a slighter large road. Turn right and look immediately to the left, towards a bowling green and a boules court (see walk 3). Keep the hall to the right. In winter, with no leaves on the trees, the view of Bramall is magnificent. Follow the steep track.

7. Approach a set of gates. Pass through these and then turn sharp right to reach the hall and gardens. The hall is only open at weekends during the winter but the gardens and tea rooms are open all the year.

8. From the Hall turn right and then right again into the restaurant and tea rooms. After a rest and a brew (take time to read the Bramall Hall Guide book) turn right into the gardens.

9. Pass through the garden with its arches of trees. Continue onwards and pass a picnic area and children's play area to the right.

Return to the car park.

Walk 18: Around Sale Water Park

Directions: Follow the M60 to Junction 6 and turn off. Sale Water Park and the Trafford Water Sports Centre are well-signed and are reached along Rifle Road. There is a free car park at the Visitors' Centre. There is also a café but this is not open on Mondays.

Special notes: Between 2004 and 2006 an extensive widening of the M60 is taking place. It is expected that, apart from at peak periods, disruption will be at a minimum. Those who enjoy shopping as well as strolling should know that Junction 10 off the M60 leads to the Trafford Centre.

Public Transport: This is not easy but the Metro-Link leads from Manchester to the Trafford Centre and although it adds a couple of miles to the walk it is not a problem for those with energy.

Map Reference: OS Explorer 277 Grid Reference 801 928

Distance: 3½ miles

Time: Allow 2½ hours

When the M63 (now the M60) was being constructed the extraction of gravel and hard core left huge holes in the ground. Those at Sale and nearby Chorlton were allowed to flood and excellent water parks were created.

Sale Water Park occupies 4.5 acres (16 hectares) and sandwiched between its banks and the motorway is a Water Sports Centre. This offers sailing, canoeing, wind surfing, angling and model boating.

The Visitors' Centre is a separate enterprise and staffed by helpful wardens. Free leaflets are available pointing out footpaths around the Sale Water Park but also the equally impressive Chorlton Water Park, which is only about one mile away. The energetic stroller could easily do both in one day but this is obviously easier on the longer days of summer. This walk only covers the Sale Water Park. Sale Water Park: 0161 881 5639. Chorlton Water Park: 0161 905 1100.

The Route

1. From the Visitors' Centre car park, turn right to the café and then through a neat little picnic area. Descend a set of wooden steps and turn right again. Pass one of a number of 'Health Trail' signs, which

The Visitors' Centre

are short circular strolls designed to provide exercise for people who need to be encouraged to walk to keep fit.

2. Follow what is obviously the main track and look for a wooden platform on the right. This leads into a Nature Reserve reached by a short wooden track. Explore this before returning to the main path. Ignore a 'Health Walk' to the right and another footpath to the left. Continue straight ahead.

3. Approach the bank of the water park. Here there is an option as there are two parallel paths. In good weather bear left through a stile and keep to the bank with the water park on the left. In wet or icy conditions follow the wider parallel track. Pass inlets to the left. The M60 and the Water Sports Centre can be seen through gaps across the water park .

4. Pass wooden seats on the right and you cannot miss the electric pylons straight ahead. At a pylon ignore the path straight ahead. Bear right through a small car park and then over a cattle grid. Bear left and follow an incline up onto the bank of the Mersey.

5. Turn left and keep the canalised Mersey to the right. Again there are two parallel paths. The lower grassy route is closer to the river

than the upper but more solid track. See and listen to an impressive little weir.

6. Find a sign indicating Broad Ees Dole Nature Reserve on the left. Explore this and use the bird hide before returning to the Mersey Bank. The word Ees (pronounced 'eyes') means a water meadow. This is a sure sign that before flood prevention schemes were devised the Mersey Valley hereabouts was often awash. There are many 'ees' in the area, including some along the present route.

7. Continue along the obvious route. Approach the busy Metro-link transport line. At Barfoot, there are three bridges over the Mersey. Furthest away is an aqueduct carrying the Bridgewater Canal over the river, then comes the tram link bridge and the closest is a foot-bridge.

8. Turn right over this footbridge and then sharp right. Cross a stile leading into Stretford Ees, which consists of pasture and hay mead-ows. The Mersey is now on the right. Again there is a choice of an upper and lower route.

9. Follow the upper track, which leads to what at first seems to be a disused reservoir. This is the 'dry weir' and was completed in 1841 by the Bridgewater Canal Company. They built a channel to allow floodwater to run to the Mersey. This avoided a repetition of the flood, which destroyed a bridge and caused considerable damage on 17th August 1840.

10. Cross the Trans-Pennine Way footpath and turn right over a bridge that crosses Chorlton Brook, which merges into the Mersey close by. Continue to follow the bank of the Mersey, which is still on the right. Many walks in this present book follow or cross the Trans-Pennine Way, which connects the east and west coasts. For details ring 01226 772574.

11. On the left is Chorlton Ees Nature Reserve, which is extensive and has a circular footpath running round it. If you are still full of energy follow this but otherwise continue along the riverside path.

Chorlton Ees occupies the site of Withington Sewage Works, which operated for more than a century before inefficiency caused its closure in 1972. A re-located works has resulted in an improve-ment in water quality. The reed beds are full of bird life in all

Walk 18. Sale Water Park

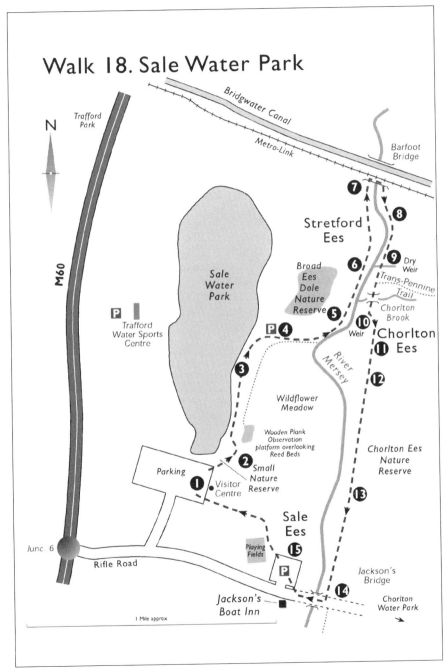

seasons and from the riverside path wooden steps lead down into the reserve.

12. Look across the river to the right where there is a wildflower meadow and an area set aside as a field enjoyed by model aeroplane enthusiasts. Those wishing to explore these areas on the opposite bank will find a footpath signed from the Visitors' Centre.

13. Approach another entrance to Chorlton Ees Nature Reserve to the left. Continue straight ahead and cross a concrete bridge.

14. Continue ahead and find a large finger post to the left. This indicates that Chorlton Water Park is only one mile along the Mersey Bank. This route, however, turns right over a substantial metal bridge over the Mersey. Beyond this on the left is Jackson's Boat Inn and the Mersey forms the old county boundary between Cheshire and Lancashire.

Jackson's Boat was once just that – a chain operated ferryboat across the Mersey. Who Jackson was, nobody seems to know – but the inn at least has a unique name. Once known as The Greyhound, and then as the Bridge Inn following the construction of the toll bridge in 1816, the unique name of Jackson's Boat has stuck – though the inn sign depicts a steamboat reminiscent of the Mississippi!

The Inn was an important haunt of Jacobites in the days when it was isolated. Supporters of Bonnie Prince Charlie met at the Inn before joining in the ill-fated 1745 rebellion. Until late Victorian times, the Inn was also a meeting place for cock fighting.

15. At Jackson's Boat turn right through an extensive car park and keep the playing fields to the left. Look for a sign indicating Sale Ees. Turn left here along a wide track and through woodland. Keep bearing left and return to the Visitors' Centre.

Walk 19: The Mersey at Warrington

Directions: The walk begins from Paddington Bank and reached from the centre of Warrington along the A57 and close to the junction with the A50. Parking is very limited but public transport is good.

Public Transport: Warrington Central Station is close to the Bus Station. Frequent buses run to Paddington Bank. Bus information: 01244 602 666. Rail information: 0151 236 7676

Map Reference: OS Explorer 276 Grid Reference 632 895

Distance: 4½ miles

Time: Allow 2½ hours

This walk cuts into the heart of old industrial Warrington, which is showing real signs of regeneration. Part of the route follows the Mersey Way, which is destined to become another major attraction.

Still regarded as an industrial town, Warrington's origins are ancient. It was a vital route over the Mersey and there are reminders of a Roman occupation in the form of artefacts now displayed in the Municipal Museum and Art Gallery on Bold Street.

The Normans knew the value of the Warrington crossing and constructed a wooden bridge, which was rebuilt in 1364 and replaced in 1495. The bridge is still a place to stand and watch the flow of the river. Look out for evidence of moorings once used to secure sailing ships. Until the 19th century, Warrington made a substantial living from the production of sailcloth. During the Industrial Revolution Warrington also produced many miles of steel wire. Before being named the 'Wolves' the Rugby League Club was known as the 'Wires'. Their ground was called Wilderspool but a new venue has been opened in 2004. Rugby League is also now a summer game but many old Wires do regret the old days of rain and mud!

The Route

1. At the gate of Paddington Bank find an obvious track leading to the Mersey. Turn upstream along the Mersey Way. The path loops around a sweeping meander. Look out for a long disused navigation known as the Woolston Old Cut. Before the Manchester Ship Canal was opened in 1894 the Woolston Cut was a vital section of the Mersey and Irwell Navigation, which opened in 1821.

2. Look carefully at the Paddington area because here was once a feeder channel to the Black Bear Canal, which was named after the existing public house (01925 418423). The line of the canal now passes through the Black Bear Country Park (see point 9).

The canal was only 8 miles long and built in 1804 to avoid negotiating an awkward tidal stretch of the Mersey between Warrington and Runcorn. After the Manchester Ship Canal was built, only a mile of the earlier canal remained important, this being the section which linked Stockton Heath swing bridge to the Mersey. This remained in use and carried cargoes of Argentinian hides to tanneries at Howley before these closed in the 1960s. In 1981, Warrington Borough Council realised that the area was potentially dangerous and converted it into the attractive park, which we now see.

3. Leaving behind the old workings it is still possible to see that this was once rich agricultural land but the effects of industry are also in evidence. The Grey Mist Pond for example was once the vital water supply for lots of factories. It is now the haunt of anglers and naturalists.

4. After this touch of Grey Mist turn right and pass Woolston new and old weirs, which have long controlled the flow of the Mersey. These are therefore vital places to visit for students of the Mersey. The river is much cleaner these days and, as the weirs agitate the water, oxygen is bubbled in and wildlife thrives. Near the old weir, look out for the few remnants of the gunpowder works built in 1755 and later destroyed by an explosion in 1853.

5. Follow the obvious route parallel to the village of Thelwall. It has, however, been somewhat savaged first by the Manchester Ship Canal and recently by the Thelwall viaduct, which carries the busy M6 over both the Ship Canal and the Mersey.

6. When the Ship Canal was excavated, huge masses of earth were piled up; the flattened tops of these are now grassed over and look natural and attractive. The area has become an important wildlife refuge.

From the largest of the 'Eyes' cross the river via a sturdy little bridge and descend to the Ship Canal. Turn right and ensure that the tiny

Walk 19. Black Bear and Thelwall

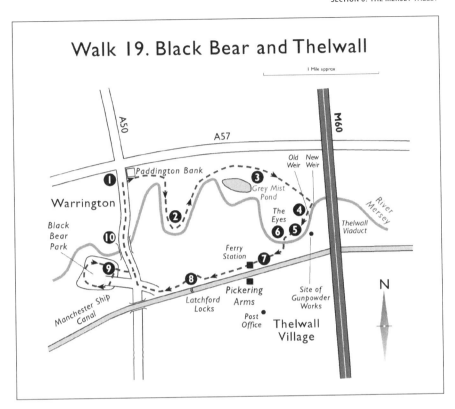

Thelwall Ferry is not missed. In ancient times the ferry crossed the Mersey but it now provides the link between the Ship Canal and Thelwall village, an important settlement in Saxon times which should not be missed.

7. The name Thelwall means a "pool by a plank bridge" and derives from Old English. It is stated that Edward the Elder founded the settlement in AD 923; an inscription on the wall of The Pickering Arms (01925 261001) records this fact.

Edward the Elder (cAD 870-AD 924) was a son of Alfred the Great and was King of Wessex from AD 899 to AD 924 and of Mercia from AD 918 to his death in AD 924. He worked with his sister Aethelfleda to establish strongholds, called *burghs*, against the Danes. One of these was at Thelwall and there was another at Widnes (see walk 21).

The last row boat: ferry across the Mersey

There are some pleasant half-timbered houses, but the Normans probably recognised Thelwall as a Saxon stronghold and they were determined not to develop it, as it may have become a site of resistance against the Normans. The ferry is a rowing boat and operates daily except Sundays. A trip on this boat is essential to get the feeling of a real 'ferry across the Mersey' – even if it is across the Ship Canal at this point.

8.   Return from the ferry and follow the track alongside the Ship Canal, on the left, and carry on to Latchford Locks. Just beyond the locks, go up to the busy A50 road.

9.   At the bridge over the Mersey look for the Black Bear Canal to the left. Even the locals refer to this now disused canal as the Black Bear but its proper name is the Runcorn and Latchford Canal. During the construction of the Manchester Ship Canal the Black Bear was gradually filled in, but the line of its route remains obvious.

10.   This walk ends by crossing the Black Bear Bridge and then returning to Paddington Bank situated on the right.

Walk 20: St Helens Canal and Sankey Brook

Directions: Follow the M6 and turn off at Junction 23 at Haydock Racecourse. Follow the A49 towards Newton-le-Willows. Turn off westwards along the A572 into Newton and then follow signs for Earlstown station. There is car parking (signed) near the centre. Earlstown and Vulcan are both part of Newton-le-Willows and were developed because of the Railway Age. Before this, Newton-le-Willows was just a quiet village.

Public Transport: This walk starts and ends at Earlstown station, which is served by Merseytravel and is on the main line between Manchester and Liverpool; tel: 0151 236 7676.

Map reference: OS Explorer 275 Grid Reference 572 953

Distance: 4½ miles including diversion to Vulcan

Time: 3 hours

Many people confuse the St Helens Canal with the Sankey Brook, which is quite understandable as the canal does run parallel to the line of the brook. The Brook once provided water for the canal. The major source of water, however, was the Carr Mill Dam, which nowadays offers a magnificent haven for wildlife and waterfowl. This is well worth a walk in its own right.

This present walk follows part of the canal towpath and passes close to Vulcan, an historic industrial village – a delightful mixture of history, natural history, industrial archaeology and surprisingly impressive stretches of countryside

Newton-le-Willows developed because it was half way between Liverpool and Manchester. When the railway came in 1830 the primitive locomotives needed coal, water, servicing and often repair at a halfway point. By 1835 Charles Tayleur, encouraged by George Stephenson, built a foundry, which became known as Vulcan. Workers' cottages were built and are now kept in splendid repair. The works only closed in June 2003 (when it was producing marine engines) and there are plans in hand to build houses and offices on the old works. This will not affect the conservation area or the route of the walk described here.

The Route

1. From the Railway Hotel turn left and pass over the railway bridge. Bear right passing a recycling centre and then bear right again to the Red Brow Car Park. Have courage at this point because the early stages of this walk are not at all impressive.

2. An obvious path crosses the canal via a swing bridge. Turn almost immediately left and follow the waterway. Opened in 1757 the original Sankey Navigation became the first still-water canal in England. Only recently has this fact been recognised, and many historians still regard the Bridgewater as the first canal (see walks 9 and 21).

3. Follow the towpath and look to the left to see Old Hey Wood and Hey Lock. At this point it is possible to enjoy a short diversion over the canal to get a closer view of Old

Sign at Vulcan Cottage

Hey Wood and the fascinating Vulcan village. This can be reached via the Vulcan locks and should not be missed.

The houses which make up the conservation area, and which surround the small village green, are very attractive. A plaque on one gable end shows the Vulcan Foundry coat of arms dated to a works extension in 1907 and another warns that no beggars or 'ballad singers' will be allowed in the village.

The Vulcan Arms ignores this directive because there is often entertainment on offer along with an impressive menu and a friendly atmosphere (01925 222314). The locals here have than a soft spot for the works and following its closure photographs of the works have been donated to the pub and proudly hang on its walls.

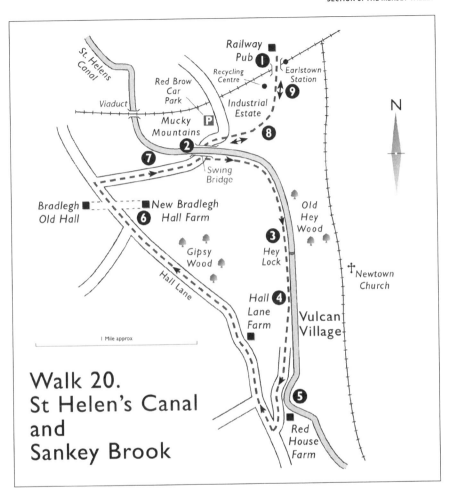

Walk 20.
St Helen's Canal
and
Sankey Brook

Nearby is the church at Newton-le-Willows. Close to the porch is the tomb inscription of a worker named Piers Naylor. This reads:

My Engine now is cold and still
No Water does my Boiler Fill
My Coke affords its Flame no More
My days of Usefulness are O'er

4. Returning to the canal via Vulcan locks suggests its days of useful-ness may also be o'er but its restoration has produced what amounts to a linear nature reserve. In the context of the 21st century this is very useful indeed! This was not, however, the original

intention of Henry Berry, who drew up the canal plans in 1755 – but he would be proud to see that his cut has survived. Berry's name deserves to be uttered in the same breath as that of Brindley, Telford and others.

Whatever the season, this is now a wonderful area for naturalists – with breeding moorhen and coot, resident mute swans and an occasional sighting of kingfisher. A pond dip reveals many species of insect and crustacean.

5. Continue for a short distance and then bear right across the Sankey Brook to reach Hall Lane beside Red House Farm.

6. Turn right along the lane. Pass by Hall Lane Farm and see Gypsy Wood to the right. At an obvious junction bear right and pass between New Bradlegh Hall Farm and Bradlegh Old Hall, which is very old indeed. Here is a moat and an impressive 15th-century gatehouse on the left. Its sheer strength shows its importance during this period.

7. Continue along the path to find impressive views of the Sankey Railway Viaduct, which is still in regular use. The viaduct is one of the great monuments of the golden periods of the railway age. It was built by George and Robert Stephenson using a construction of sandstone blocks and bricks, which they completed in 1830. This was the first bridge to carry a commercial railway over a commercial waterway. It has long been known locally as the Nine Arches and cost only £45,000. Those who choose to park at Red Brow car park (see stop 8) will notice that it was an old quarry. The sandstone for the viaduct came from this source.

Look to the right of the viaduct and view what is left of the Sankey Sugar Refinery, which processed raw cane sugar from 1869 to 1979.

8. Return to Red Brow Car Park and along Earle Street to the station. This and indeed Earlstown itself is named in memory of Sir Hardman Earle – another famous railway engineer of the 1850s. At first the station was called Newton Junction but it was later changed to Earlstown.

Walk 21: St Helens Canal and Spike Island

Directions: The site of Spike Island and the Mersey exit from the Sankey Canal is now explained by exhibits in the Catalyst Chemical Museum. This can be reached via the M57 and A5300 from Liverpool. It is reached from Cheshire via the M56 and over the Runcorn Bridge. Brown signs indicate the car park, which is free. Museum telephone number: 0151 420 1121

Public Transport There are bus services to Widnes from St Helens and Liverpool and a Merseyrail station; tel: 0151 236 7676

Map Reference: OS Explorer 275 Grid Reference 515 845

Distance: 3½ miles linear with a linking bus service at the far end at Fiddlers Ferry. This area is so important in terms of Mersey's history that I always retrace my steps. The walk is therefore 7 miles.

Time: Allow 3½ hours

Once a health resort blessed by the name Montpelier, Runcorn is said to have no history before the Industrial Revolution. What an insult! It is said that there was a fortification built by King Alfred's daughter Aethelfleda in AD 915 (see walk 19). The dynasty needed these defensive settlements close to river crossings to keep the invading Danes at bay.

It is also thought that Augustinian monks established a small priory at Widnes before moving to a better location across the Mersey at Norton (see walk 12). The Runcorn Gap was a vital crossing point as it was at the narrowest point along this stretch of the Mersey. This walk is now full of wildlife and scenery sandwiched between the St Helens (Sankey) Canal and the tidal flats of the Mersey.

The Route

1. As visitors flow towards the Catalyst Museum, young and old picnic on the seats provided which overlook the estuary and boaters lounge on their brightly painted vessels. It is hard to realise that Spike Island was once one of the most polluted areas in the world. The word Spike actually means a 'doss house' – a lurid description of the appalling conditions in which the workers had to live.

The Industrial Revolution demanded more and more alkali, and Spike Island provided it. You cannot make soap or glass without alkali and neither can textiles be finished without this vital group of chemicals. In the early days, these essential chemicals could only be produced by the backbreaking business of collecting seaweed, which was then burned to produce the vital sodium and potassium salts. The industry was initially based in coastal areas. Once chemists learned to synthesise alkalis raw materials could be imported and derivatives exported via estuaries. This area of the Mersey estuary therefore became world famous and the history is well told in the displays mounted in the catalyst museum. The views over the estuary from the top floor of the museum are magnificent.

2. The Ranger Cabin has displays of history and natural history and the friendly staff are always ready to explain the essential features of the Sankey Canal.

More accurately referred to as the St Helens Canal the navigation was created by cutting a route from the Mersey at Widnes and led to Sankey Bridge near Warrington. There was a new entry into the river at Fiddlers Ferry in 1764 and another at Widnes itself in 1830 but still it never became part of the main canal system. It has ten locks, ran for eight miles and opened in 1757, two years before the Bridgewater was started. Its original intention was to connect the huge St Helens coalfield with the Mersey at Fiddler's Ferry. This is why the St Helens is not regarded as the first canal, but why this should be is at least open to question.

3. The West Bank Boat Club proves that once a disused canal is restored it can play a vital role in the tourist industry. The colourful barges and pleasure craft look almost as graceful as the large numbers of mute swans, which are now resident hereabouts along with kingfishers and heron. What a contrast to the days when the heavy pall of industrial smog smothered Spike Island.

4. The bridge over the canal is the perfect place to enjoy the movement of the boats. Then follow the fringes of a woodland and some impressive areas of grass.

This bridge is now made of wood but a more substantial structure long dismantled once carried a railway over onto Spike Island. A

Walk 21. Sankey Canal and Spike Island

Fiddlers Ferry Power Station

St. Helens Canal

Locks

8

N

Lagoons

6 **7**

5

West Bank Boat Club **3**

4

9

2

Spike Island

Ranger Cabin

1

Tidal Area

Widnes

Catalyst Museum

Locks

10

River Mersey

Runcorn Widnes Bridge

Runcorn Gap

Runcorn

Manchester Ship Canal

Docks

1 Mile approx

careful look will reveal signs of the earlier iron construction and the roller mechanism, which operated the capstan to turn the swing bridge.

5. Carter House Bridge is now a fixed crossing but it was also a swing bridge at one time. Nearby is Bowers Brook, which was diverted to its present course when the Spike Island complex was reclaimed from what was a marshy area. A look to the right especially in winter will reveal a host of marshland birds including shelduck, wigeon, curlew and several species of small wader.

6. Cuerdley Marsh and Johnsons Crossing are other examples of the perfect balance between industrial archaeology and natural history.

Johnsons was formerly yet another swing bridge and, at one time, a large sewer pipe crossed the canal and then led into the Mersey, discharging directly into the river. United Utilities have dealt with this problem (and many others in the area) and the quality of the water is now high enough to support more and more invertebrates, which in turn supports fish and bird life.

7. The lagoons are refuges for large numbers of birds throughout the year but especially in the colder months of the year. The canal at this point has suffered from silting, but restoration is now well in hand. This is a perfect place to birdwatch and picnic, while watching the Mersey as it narrows towards the Widnes-Runcorn gap.

The word Widnes comes from two Norse words – Vide meaning 'wide' and Ness meaning 'nose'. This refers to the wide section of the Mersey just before the narrowing at the Runcorn Gap.

Overlooking the lagoons across the canal is the coal-fired Fiddler's Ferry Power Station, which opened in 1957. The lagoons are actually settling ponds connected to the power station across the canal and via a bridge.

8. Fiddler's Ferry lock system marks the end of this linear walk but the return journey is well worth the effort because if the timing is right the estuary changes with the ebb and flow of the tide.

Originally there were two locks, which were designed to speed up the movement of Mersey Flat Vessels between the river and the canal. This system was in operation until 1846 when the construction of the railway meant the realignment of the canal.

9. After lots of fascinating bird watching a left turn opposite to the bridge at Point 4 leads directly onto the Mersey bank. A look onto the sands (now much cleaner) reveals all that is left of some Mersey Flats embedded in the mud and seen at low tides. These vessels are no longer afloat and to the right of the footpath is a fine example of a rudder of a Mersey Flat.

10. The locks at Spike Island are overlooked by the Catalyst Chemical Museum which is a very modern building describing a very old industry.

Across the bridge is a footpath indicating that this area is part of the Trans-Pennine Trail and indicates Fiddler's Ferry Marina. It also points to another walk leading to Pickerings Pasture, a linear distance of 2 miles. Here is another example of how the Mersey's environment has improved. No botanist should miss this place. In summer both the walk described here and Pickerings Pasture can easily be covered in one day.

For students of the Mersey, the Spike Island area has greater interest than almost anywhere along the whole course of the catchment. Here, too, are splendid views of

A Mersey Flat in 1900

the Runcorn Bridge – now one of the major crossings over the Mighty Mersey. It is hoped that the new crossing to be built upstream will take some of this traffic congestion away from this bridge.

SECTION 7: THE CHESHIRE BANK

Any account of the Cheshire bank of the Mersey must devote space to the Weaver, which is a major tributary. Over the last two thousand years, but particularly in the last two centuries, the Weaver has given its life to the salt trade. To begin a study of the river, the stroller must ascend to a lofty perch up on the Mersey View and look at Frodsham and Weston villages. These are sited on either side of the Weaver as it merges into the Ship Canal and the Mersey (see walk 23). Look for the Weaver Bends, an area rightly famous in the ornithological world, before rambling upstream in search of Weaverham and Northwich. Look for the very recently restored Anderton Boat Lift (see walk 22).

Any industry depends upon good transport and salt was no exception. A look at OS maps of the area reveals old salt roads (many absorbed by the modern A49) and names such as Salterswell, Salterford, and Salthouses which are self-explanatory.

Until the Industrial Revolution many villages along the Weaver, although producing salt on a limited scale were largely undisturbed by what we now know as modern commerce. Then salt became vital to the development of the chemical industry and a Weaver River Navigation became essential. Thus the gently meandering Weaver was straightened so rigidly that it is more reminiscent of a canal than a river. The Frodsham marshes, however, were never completely tamed and a deep canal was cut to link with the Mersey at Weston Point. A major dock was constructed as early as 1810.

Today the whole length of the Weaver estuary area is a complex of artificial waterways and affords many opportunities to stroll through history and natural history. Daresbury church has firm connections with Charles Dodgson (1832-1898) alias Lewis Carroll, whose father was rector of the church. Here too is the Atomic Research establishment and nearby is Norton Priory (see walk no.12) which, along with Birkenhead Priory, controlled the rowboat ferries across the Mersey. This is why we still pay tolls on the Cheshire side of the tunnels.

The River of Salt provides plenty of strolls and there are equally attractive rambles along the Cheshire bank of the Mersey itself.

The Cheshire Bank

It is difficult to imagine how remote this area must have been before industrial development. There would have been flat sands, salmon fishing, unpolluted rivers and three monasteries. Norton and Birkenhead controlled the ferries, whilst the Cistercians at Stanlow had a much less attractive site. The area kept flooding and, by the 14th century, they abandoned their abbey and relocated to Whalley where haunting ruins still stand close to the confluence of the Ribble and the Lancashire Calder. The only haunting thing about Stanlow nowadays is the petrochemical complex that lines the Cheshire bank of the Mersey (see walk 6).

Industry, however, did not obliterate all the countryside as provided by Eastham Country Park (see walk 24). In some cases the impact of industry was very positive and the Ellesmere Port Boat Museum is a valuable and much loved tourist location (see walk 6).

Here, too, is the world-famous Unilever empire and no visitor to the Mersey should miss the village built for his workers by William Hesketh Lever. Its real attraction can only be seen on foot (see walk 25).

A combination of an increased and more affluent population plus glorious scenery cries out for development and New Brighton was just that – a resort on the Mersey to rival the Prince Regent's (later George IV) Brighton (see walk 26).

To those interested in maritime history, New Brighton is much more interesting than Brighton in Sussex, for the Liverpool skyline and docks as seen from the Cheshire bank are as spectacular as anywhere in the world.

Walk 22: The Weaver and The Anderton Boat Lift

Directions: From the M6 turn off at Junction 19. Follow the B5391 towards Northwich. Brown signs indicate the Anderton Lift. An alternative route is via the M56 turning off at Junction 10. Follow the A49 to Barnton from which the lift is well signed. Follow the narrow track with its traffic calmers to the Operations Centre of the lift, where there is a large free car park; tel: 01606 786777 or go to www.andertonboatlift.co.uk

The centre is sandwiched between the Trent and Mersey Canal, the River Weaver and the Weaver navigation. The Operations Centre is open daily from 09.45 to 17.00 hours. There is an entry fee and with an extra charge for those who want to board the trip boat which takes passengers up and down the lift. There is a shop, restaurant and exhibitions – many of which are 'hands on'.

Map reference: OS Explorer 267 Grid Reference 648 756

Distance: 6 miles

Time: 3 hours

For more than a century, walkers have been fascinated by the mix of spectacularly beautiful countryside and unique industrial archaeology to be found between the Trent and Mersey Canal and the River Weaver with its associated navigation.

Not for nothing has the Weaver been known as the River of Salt. From Roman times the area now known as Cheshire was exploited for its salt and part of a soldier's wages was paid in essential salt. This was his *salarium* – from which 'salary' is derived.

The Anderton Lift, known as the *Cathedral of the Canals*, was the first of its type to be built in the world. Edwin Clark's masterpiece began operations in 1875 and its function was to speed up cargoes between the Trent and Mersey Canal and the River Weaver, which provided access to the Mersey and the sea. The height difference between the upper canal and the lower Weaver was only 50 feet, but the lift meant cargoes mainly of salt and pottery did not have to be loaded and unloaded. The vessels were transported bodily in huge caissons filled with water.

In 1983 the lift was considered unsafe and closed but a Lottery Grant in 1998 of £3.3 million was added to matching funds and the £7 million project began. British Waterways finished the project in 2002 and it is now very impressive. Since the 2003 season it has been possible to use the lift as a focus for a number of Weaverside wanderings.

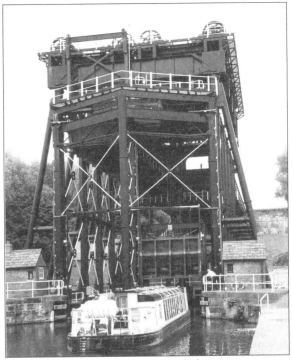

The Anderton Boat Lift

The Route

1. From the car park head slightly downhill to the towpath of the Trent and Mersey Canal. Turn left towards Bridge Number 199.

The Trent and Mersey's construction resulted in a demand from the Staffordshire potteries and, in 1765, Josiah Wedgwood wanted to link the Trent and the Mersey. It is not difficult to imagine how difficult it was to transport delicate pottery by horse and cart on rough roads. The industry around Tunstall, Hanley, Stoke, Fenton and Longton was first called 'The Potteries' but the area is now known collectively as Stoke-on-Trent. As business increased, Cornish clay was needed in large quantities and this came via the Mersey and the Weaver, but the last lap had to be by horse and cart.

In May 1766 a Canal Act passed through Parliament and by May 1777 the Trent and Mersey was open along its length of 93 miles. The only difficult part of the journey was at Anderton where the

Weaver and the Canal ran parallel but the Trent and Mersey was high above the river. The ground proved too unstable for locks to work but it was almost a century before engineers were able to devise the lift.

2. On the left is the entrance to the operations centre with its passenger trip boat jetties and the River Weaver, which is overlooked by the sprawling chemical works of Brunner-Mond. Follow the obvious route down to the river and embark on the trip boat, which lifts its passengers up to the Trent and Mersey. Look out for pieces of machinery associated with old workings in the life of the lift. Look out to the left to see, and hear, a channel of excess water running down from the canal to the river.

3. Follow the path to the trip boat. This is named Edwin Clark after the designer and was converted from a former maintenance craft, which once worked on the Leeds and Liverpool Canal near Burnley.

Whilst the vessel is moving, a running commentary explains the history of the lift. When waiting for the trip to start, this is the best place to understand just how important the Weaver was to the salt trade. The Brunner Mond works is still salt-based and the chutes, which operated before the lift was built, can still be seen.

Until the 17th century all goods passing into and through this area were transported overland. The influential and increasingly wealthy salt merchants were demanding that the River Weaver should be canalised. In 1721 an Act was passed by parliament and, by 1734, a 20-mile stretch from the Mersey via Frodsham and up to Winsford was operational. A further Act passed in 1759 meant that the Weaver navigation was able to generate good profits. The basin at Anderton was set up and this accounts for the lift being in its present-day position.

4. Alight from the trip boat on the Trent and Mersey and then, keeping the lift to the left, follow the towpath over the bridge. If you are hungry or thirsty, cross over the bridge to reach the Stanley Arms (01606 75059). The name celebrates Sir John Stanley who, in 1793, sold land on which salt chutes could be built to deliver salt from the canal down to the river. This pub offers a good menu, serves morn-

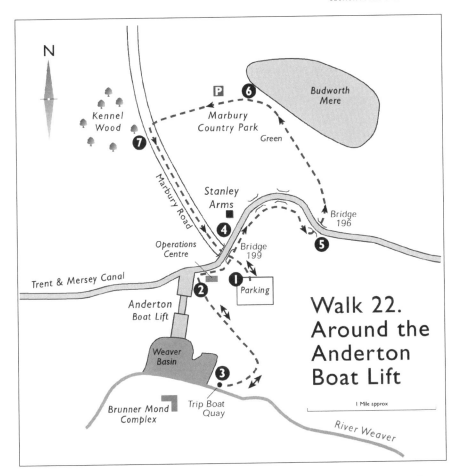

N

Kennel
Wood

Marbury
Country Park

Budworth
Mere

Green

Marbury Road

Stanley
Arms

Bridge
196

Operations
Centre

Bridge
199

Trent & Mersey Canal

Parking

Anderton
Boat Lift

Weaver
Basin

Walk 22.
Around the
Anderton
Boat Lift

Brunner Mond
Complex

Trip Boat
Quay

I Mile approx

River Weaver

ing coffee and bar snacks and is close to a small landing stage from which trip boats operate along the canal.

5. From the Stanley Arms cross the bridge and turn left along the towpath. Find bridge number 196 and left turn into Marbury Park. It was here that rock salt was first discovered. This was in 1670 when engineers were mining in search of coal.

The meres in this area were scraped out by the retreating glaciers at the conclusion of the last Ice Age. Marbury village is situated at the end of the Big Mere. Here there is a cluster of cottages, the pleasant Swan Inn and the church of St Michael. This is set high on a natural mound and most of its architecture dates to the 13th century. Look for the village green and a commemorative tree planted to celebrate Wellington's victory at Waterloo in 1815.

6. Marbury Country Park consists of 200 acres (80 hectares) of land which once belonged to the Smith-Berry family and which overlooks Budworth mere. Sadly Marbury Hall was demolished in 1968 but the park now has an excellent information centre surrounded by picnic tables; tel: 01606 77741.

7. From the Park with its network of footpaths continue past the car park on the right. Turn left along Marbury Road and explore Kennel Wood, on the right. Continue to bridge 199. Turn right and return to the Boat Lift car park.

An extension for the energetic

From bridge 196 follow the canal footpath to bridge 193 and visit the Lion Saltworks. The Thompson family began rock salt mining in 1856 behind the Red Lion Hotel. The Lion Saltworks expanded and the hotel was eventually demolished as new pan houses were constructed. Salt was shipped by canal via the Anderton Lift and thence to Liverpool, Manchester, Canada, America, Africa and India.

The Thompsons worked the traditional way until their Lion Saltworks ceased to roar in 1986. The Vale Royal Borough Council prevented demolition and a charitable trust now operates the salt works; tel: 01606 41823.

The longish trek back to the lift passes Great Budworth on the right and Budworth Mere and Marbury Park on the left. Return via Marbury Road making a round total of around 10 miles.

Postscript

British Waterways have been advised by the Government to make more use of canals. By 2005 or perhaps earlier heavy non-perishable cargoes may be using this waterway system and the lift in order to reduce heavy traffic congestion. Most people including the author welcome this development, but these political promises have been made before.

Walk 23: Frodsham, the Weaver and the Mersey View

Directions: Follow the M56 and exit at Junction 12. Follow the signs for Frodsham. Cross a substantial metal bridge over the Weaver and continue along the A56 into Frodsham. There are car parks and some street parking. The Bear's Paw is on the main road close to a set of traffic lights.

Public Transport: There is a rail link with regular services from Chester and Liverpool into Frodsham. From Easter to the end of October there is a Sandstone Rambler bus (NO 85) that runs between Frodsham, Delamere and Whitchurch each weekend and on Bank Holidays. Contact Cheshire Traveline: 01244 602666.

Map Reference: OS Explorer 266 & 275 Grid Reference 518 770. *The Sandstone Trail* is a free leaflet describing a 34-mile (55km) walk from Frodsham to Whitchurch. The present walk follows the initial section of this route. For full details ring 08457 603456.

Distance: 5 miles

Time: 3 hours to allow for exploration

Warning: Part of the track up to the Mersey View is steep and can be slippery after rain or frost. Appropriate footwear should be worn.

This route provides panoramic views of the confluence of the Weaver and the Mersey set amidst a complex of chemical works. These look surprisingly attractive especially in the dark as flames and multicoloured lights caress the sky.

Where the Weaver bends meet the Mersey has long been a Mecca for birdwatchers. Despite the presence of industry thousands of resident and migrant birds are present with keen watchers on the look out for rarities. Birds such as peregrine, merlin and buzzard are regularly seen and in spring and autumn rarities such as greenshank are seen more regularly than in most areas. Flocks of common birds such as dunlin and knot now feed on the mud flats especially during the winter.

There is a footpath from Frodsham to the Weaver Bends but the present stroll starts at the Bear's Paw and winds up to the Mersey View near the attractive War Memorial.

The Route

1. Start at the Bear's Paw, which was built of sandstone in 1632 and it is stated that the cruel sport of bear baiting did go on there. In the 18th and 19th centuries the hostelry was an important stop on the coaching route. It still caters well for visitors, the food is wholesome and varied, and the beams and fires add a Georgian feel to the place; tel: 01928 731404.

2. Opposite Bear's Paw are traffic lights. Cross at this point and continue up Church Street. Look out for a footpath signed Howey Lane, which follows the marked *Sandstone Trail*. Find the church of St Lawrence on the left. This stands high over Frodsham and the site may well date back to Saxon times. There is a late 14th-century tower containing a *Hagioscope*. This is also known as a Leper's squint which is a hole allowing those with infectious diseases to watch the service without infecting the healthy. The rest of the church dates to the 15th century but there were major restorations and extensions in 1715 and between 1880 and 1883.

3. Opposite the church is the splendid Ring O' Bells pub, which is one of many "resting places" along this route; tel: 01928 732068. Cross the road to this hostelry, pass it on the right and walk up Bellemonte Road.

4. Look out for a rather small sign on the right indicating Middle Walk. This leads into deciduous woodland. Follow this and ascend a steep but well maintained track. In spring this is a naturalist's delight with flowers and bird song being special features. In winter the lack of leaves enables better views over the Mersey to be appreciated but it can be very slippery after frost.

5. The track bears left and then heads for country dominated by the splendid War Memorial – a soaring obelisk erected after World War I. Here, there are seats overlooking the confluence of the Weaver with the Mersey and also visible is the Bridgewater Canal.

    Follow the *Sandstone Trail* markers passing the Forest Hill Hotel on the left. The view from the bedrooms of this modern building must be spectacular especially at night.

6. Descend a set of steps called the Baker's Dozen into Dunsdale Hollow. Look out for the small Beacon Hill Car Park. At this point, leave the *Sandstone Trail* by turning left.

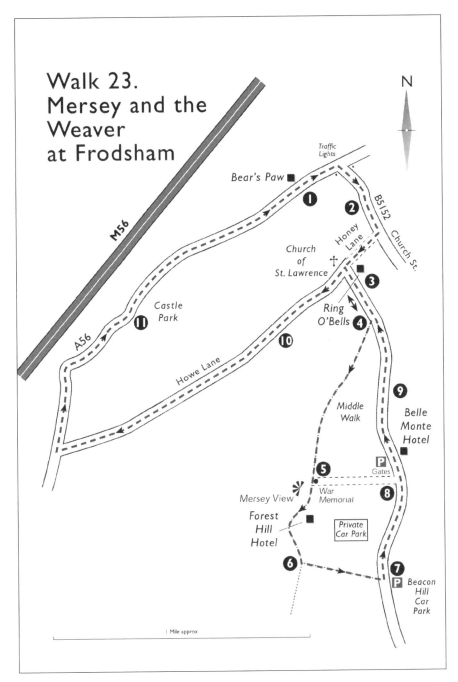

Walk 23.
Mersey and the
Weaver
at Frodsham

N

M56

A56

Castle
Park

Howe Lane

Bear's Paw ■

Traffic
Lights

B5152

Church St.

❶

❷

Honey
Lane

Church
of
St. Lawrence ✝

❸

Ring
O'Bells ❹

❺

❻

❼ P
Beacon
Hill
Car
Park

❽

❾

Belle
Monte
Hotel ■

P
Gates

Middle
Walk

War
Memorial

Private
Car Park

Mersey View

Forest
Hill
Hotel ■

⓫

⓿

1 Mile approx

7. Descend the very narrow road (take care) and find the Forest Hill Hotel and Conference Centre on the left. There is also a night-spot called The Mersey View which was once a little café and gift shop. Although this has gone, visitors still arrive here. The Mersey View is best seen from the War Memorial (see stop 4 and stop 8).

Thousands of Dunlin are found along the Weaver Bends during the colder months of the year

8. Continue the steep descent to a small car park opposite the impressive gates of the War Memorial. It is worth following the grassy track through these gates for another close look at the War Memorial and the Mersey View. This will add less than half a mile in total. The whole of this area is rich in wildlife with more than 15 species of butterfly being regularly recorded in the summer. In spring and autumn the bird count is often spectacular. The seats provide ideal picnic spots.

9. Return to the Memorial gates and continue to descend. On the left pass two more hostelries – the Belle Monte and the Bull's Head. Approach the Ring O' Bells with the church straight ahead.

10. Turn left and descend a steep road lined on either side by impressive houses. Continue downhill until you reach the A56. Turn right and then look right for Castle Park Arts Centre. Many people wonder why such a high and prominent settlement like Frodsham did not have a castle. Actually, it did – but on the 10th August 1654, the castle was destroyed by fire. Its stonework was later used in the construction of buildings, which are now known as Council Offices and Arts Centre. The castle probably had Saxon origins but its wooden structure was replaced by Norman stonework in the early 12th century. This would have been an ideal place to defend the strategic crossings over the Weaver and the Mersey.

11. After exploring the castle site turn right and continue through Frodsham to the Bear's Paw.

Walk 24: Eastham Country Park

Directions: From the M6 follow the M56 and M53. Turn off at Junction 5. Follow the A47. Look out for a brown sign indicating Eastham Country Park. There is free parking here at the 76-acre (30.4 hectare) site; tel: 0151 327 1007.

Public Transport: There is a railway station at Bromborough. This is only about one mile from the Country Park and can be reached along Allport Road.

Map Reference: OS Explorer 266 & 275 Grid Reference 365 815.

Distance: 3½ miles

Time: 2 hours

The Route

1. **The Country Park:** for centuries, only rowboat ferries linked Liverpool with the Wirral. This meant that usually only essential business trips were taken, but the coming of the steam-powered paddle steamers increased passenger numbers. Then, in the 1840s, came the railway bridge. Potential visitors were therefore sought after, especially by Thomas Stanley. By 1846 he had built gardens landscaped with rhododendrons and azaleas, plus ornamental trees and fountains. He added a zoo with a bear pit, monkey enclosures and dens for lions. He also provided a boating lake, water chute, roller coaster, bandstand, ballroom and cafés. He brought in stars such as 'Blondin, the tightrope walker' and other high profile entertainers. The pleasure grounds declined during the years following the 1914-18 war and the last pleasure paddle-steamer left Eastham pier in 1929.

The present country park is either a disaster or an asset, depending on your point of view. To my mind the walk around the well-marked paths is a wonderful tour of industrial archaeology.

The Country Park Information Centre is based in what was an old blacksmith's shop and it contains artefacts relating to the area and to the Eastham Ferry. A trail leaflet is available free. This should be followed although it does add an extra mile to the walk.

Here are found both exotic and native plants and the sound of birdsong echoes throughout the woodlands in spring. An examination of the undergrowth reveals the remains of old fountains, animal enclosures and a very well preserved bear pit. It should be remembered that the Victorians had a different view of animal welfare than is now the case.

2. **Job's Ferry** is much smaller than that at Eastham. From the old landing stage the view differs according to the state of the tide. On the ebb are mud flats, which provide food for birds such as shelduck and a wide assortment of waders. Not so long ago, these mud flats were often coated with globules of oil, but petrochemical companies now devote much time and money to reducing spills.

From Job's Ferry it is easy to remember how wild and desolate this area of the Mersey was before the onset of industry. In those days the villages of Bromborough and Eastham were isolated although linked by winding paths around the riverside and often subject to flooding.

A thousand years ago, Bromborough was the most important settlement on the Wirral, having a regular market and an annual fair. Even in Victorian times the settlement was important "owing to its natural beauty and proximity to Liverpool it has become a favourite place of residence". No doubt this popularity was due to the coming of the reliable railway link. Later came the road tunnels and the increased efficiency of transport, which led to the decline of the market. Then came the chemical industry, which also adversely affected Eastham as a village.

3. From the old cast iron **Eastham Ferry** landing stage there are panoramic views over the Mersey. To the left is the Liverpool skyline, which includes the two cathedrals and the 'Three Graces' on the Pier Head. To the right is the entrance to the Manchester Ship Canal, which opened in 1894. This led to a rapid development of the petrochemical industry in the Eastham area (see walk 6).

Easily visible from the old ferry are two hostelries – the Eastham Ferry and the Tap. Why are there two such establishments within a few yards of each other? The 'posh' Eastham Ferry Hotel was to

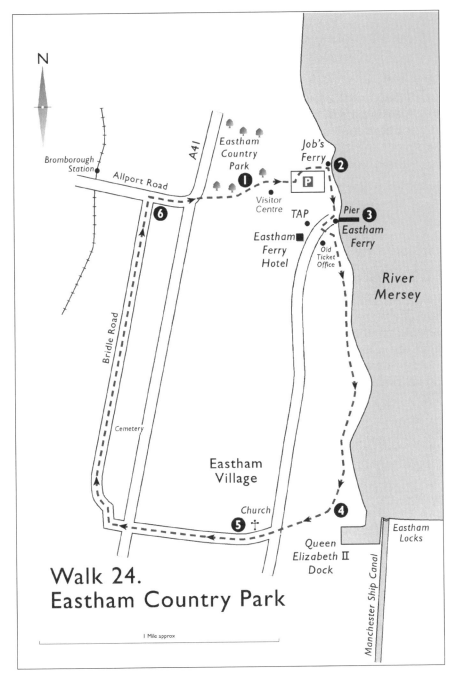

N

Bromborough
Station

Allport Road

A41

Eastham
Country
Park

Job's
Ferry

❷

❶

P

Visitor
Centre

TAP

Pier ❸

Eastham
Ferry

❻

Eastham ■
Ferry
Hotel

Old
Ticket
Office

River
Mersey

Bridle Road

Cemetery

Eastham
Village

Church

❺ ✝

❹

Queen
Elizabeth II
Dock

Eastham
Locks

Manchester Ship Canal

Walk 24.
Eastham Country Park

I Mile approx

provide for the well to do traveller whilst the Tap was used by servants, boatmen and those who tended the horses. As he was developing his Pleasure Gardens Thomas Stanley decided to build these two new hostelries which are still functioning well today.

There is a third building near the ferry that is of interest. The red sandstone ticket office, which dates from 1857, once functioned as a public toilet. The building is still standing, but the toilet is no more and it is showing signs of neglect. Something should be done to make use of the building.

4.   This is the point that provides the best view of the opening of the Manchester Ship Canal. This led to major developments around Eastham and Stanlow. Although some have suggested that the Ship Canal has totally declined this is not the case and large vessels can still move on to all points up to Manchester.

The Queen Elizabeth II dock was constructed after the 1939-45 war and this attracts many vessels serving the oil refineries. This area of Eastham is the place to watch barges, tugs and oil tankers.

5.   Eastham is a venerable village but far too many people drive through it in order to get to the Country Park. What a real joy they miss. In the churchyard is a yew tree, which some experts believe is more than 1500 years old.

Eastham was mentioned in Domesday and it was stated, "Hugh the Earl of Chester held Eastham which consisted of 22 hides". Each hide consists of 120 acres (48 hectares) and the Norman lords had been given land that had belonged to a Saxon named Edwin. This proves that Eastham was well established long before the Normans landed. Early Christians may well have worshipped under the yew tree, formerly used by pagans, and the church came later.

The village is still dominated by the magnificent church of St Mary, which is reached via a splendid lych gate. The church has a sturdy 14th-century tower but the history of the building is also of interest to naturalists!

The church warden's accounts of 1702 reveals that a bounty was paid to those who killed kites. Once regarded as a real nuisance kites are now real rarities. It is even stranger to find that the main aim was to remove the black kite, which is now extinct in Britain. It

Exhibit at the Visitor Centre

is only red kites that now occur in Britain but even this species is found in only very small numbers. Black kites feed on offal, which decreased naturally as refuse collections became more organised. The use of firearms was also devastating for many raptors.

6. The walk to this point reveals portions of new and old Merseyside. A left turn leads to Bromborough station and modern shops, cafés and pubs. In the old days Bromborough was a marshy area but new industries have wrapped themselves around Eastham. In a sense, Eastham is a sort of "Bromborough sandwich".

The right turn leads along lines of trees to the Country Park which, in terms of wildlife, has changed very little over the last few hundred years, with a few exceptions. One major exception to the fauna list is the presence of grey squirrels. In the 1870s grey squirrels were introduced from North America because it was thought to be a way of controlling red squirrels, which were then regarded as a nuisance. These days, the grey is a real pest whilst the red is now almost extinct in England.

On the day of my visit the bird list soon built up to impressive proportions but on a "one off" visit there were no rarities. Soon, however, I watched a colourful jay and a mouse like treecreeper, which climbed spirally up a tree. There was also a nuthatch, which is the only British bird that can climb headfirst down a tree trunk. My attention was drawn to a knocking sound and I found a song thrush banging a snail against an old stone. Around the stone I found many snail shells, which had been broken. Stones used like this are called anvils. I watched the thrush break the shell by hammering the snail on the anvil. The soft body was then carried away obviously to feed a nest full of young thrushes.

I spent the last stretch of my walk looking down at the Mersey estuary, which is now so unpolluted that the area has been declared as an SSSI (Site of Special Scientific Interest). The atmosphere is clean these days as chemical emissions are reduced to a minimum. I watched a swallow feeding its young around the Visitor Centre complex – see picture below.

Swallow feeding young

Walk 25: Port Sunlight

Directions: Follow M6, M56 and then the M53. From Junction 5 follow the A41 towards Birkenhead. Look out for the brown sign indicating Port Sunlight. An alternative route is via Liverpool and through the Birkenhead Tunnel. From the exit to the tunnel pay the toll on the Birkenhead side and pick up the A41. Follow the signs for Chester until the brown sign indicates Port Sunlight. There is parking all round the village but take care to respect the privacy of the residents. There is a large parking area at the Lady Lever Art Gallery.

Public Transport: There is a railway station at Port Sunlight and this is very close to the Heritage Centre (0151 236 7676). There is also a bus service from Chester, Birkenhead and New Brighton. Telephone as above.

Map Reference: OS Explorer 266 & 275 Grid Reference 340 846

Distance: 2 miles

Time: Take at least 3 hours with plenty of stops.

This is not so much a countryside ramble as a stroll through one of the prettiest villages in England. There is a distinct feeling here of a Tudor village and yet it was created from a marshland solely because of industry and one man's dream. In this sense Port Sunlight bears a superficial resemblance to Worsley (see walk 9).

Although a specific route has been followed here it would be just as sensible to wander haphazardly around Port Sunlight in search of the old Mersey Marshland. Some of these areas are indicated during the walk but there are some 'damp patches', which are not mentioned here or in the literature. Visitors need to look at Port Sunlight and think about the Mersey marshland prior to the 1880s.

An Extra Stroll

Between Port Sunlight and Bebbington is Dibbinsdale Local Nature Reserve, funded by Unilever. In 2001, I was present when this trail was visited by Prince Charles and the Queen of Denmark. Their visit was to celebrate an aspect of the cleaning up of the River Mersey and its tributaries. Details can be obtained from the Heritage Centre.

The Route

1. **Port Sunlight Station** is the place to try to imagine what the area was like before William Hesketh Lever set out in search of his ideal industrial site. Lever was born in Bolton in 1851 but, by 1885, he was based in Warrington and his ambition was to produce a brand of soap to make his fortune. He stopped using evil-smelling tallow and substituted vegetable oil that not only got rid of the stink, but also gave a smoother texture. He added citronella oil and, in a stroke of genius, he called his soap Sunlight. Soon, the old Warrington works could not produce enough of his new soap and he set out to find a site close to the Mersey and the sea. This would cut the cost of both his imports and exports.

Lever finally arrived at Bromborough Pool with an outlet leading from Lower Bebbington and out into the Mersey. He eventually developed this into a model village, which he called Port Sunlight. He may well have been inspired by another such village which was close by but on a much smaller scale. Prices Patent Candle Company had already constructed a village at Bromborough for their employees as early as 1853. The Wild Mersey was thus being tamed.

2. The Heritage Centre is the best place to explore Lever's developments, which have evolved into Unilever – now an industrial giant; tel: 0151 644 6466. Small admission charge. Open daily (except Christmas week). Between the Heritage Centre and the station are the magnificent offices of the Company.

Touring the Heritage Centre, it is easy to see that Lever was not a man to do things by halves and he had his plans worked out by 1888. He constructed 1400 houses plus 50 buildings devoted to leisure activities. He directed that no two streets were to be alike and this is why each turn of this stroll reveals something different.

The Heritage Centre sells soap, ornaments and copies of advertisements dating from the old days to the present time. There are pictures of the factory, offices and all laboratories hard at work.

Opposite the Heritage Centre is the Gladstone Theatre opened by the Victorian Prime Minister in 1891 and now run by a successful Theatre Trust. It was originally built as a recreation hall and dining room for male employees.

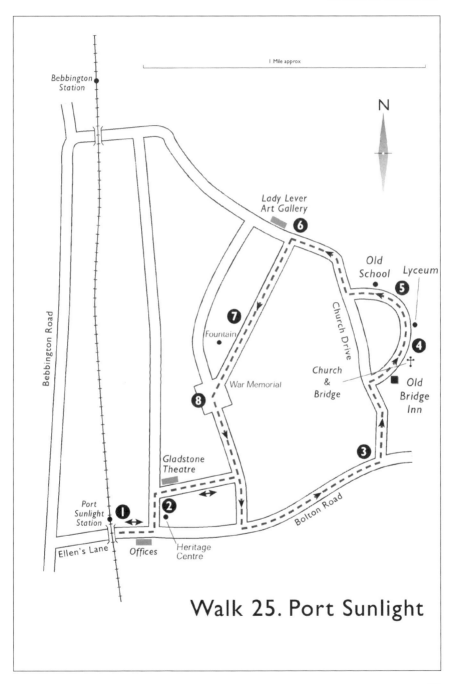

Walk 25. Port Sunlight

3. The area known as **The Dell** indicates that at one time there was a creek leading out into the Mersey. At the time when there was a marsh in this area and, at several points during this stroll there are depressions, which make this obvious.

4. The Old Bridge Inn was opened in 1900 but was not licensed. Lever proved himself not be an autocrat by allowing his employees to vote whether or not the place should serve alcohol. More than 80% said, "Yes please" and the Bridge has provided sustenance ever since. There was once a bridge over the Mersey at this site.

The Bridge was featured in the film 'Chariots of Fire' which was shot in 1981. This monument and Christ Church Parsonage is now a popular setting for weddings. The sight of vintage cars and young brides add much to the ambience of Port Sunlight.

Opposite Bridge Cottage is the Lyceum, which was built between 1894 and 1896, serving a dual function of school and church. There is now not only a social club but also a place where some of Unilever's archives are kept. The building is set around a well-kept bowling green and lawns.

Here also is Hulme Hall, which was opened as a women's dining room in 1901 and could accommodate 2000 people. Why Hulme Hall? The maiden name of Lord Leverhulme's wife was Elizabeth Ellen Hulme. It also accounts for William using the word Leverhulme in his title.This hall has its place in pop history, as it was here that Ringo Starr first played drums with the Beatles.

5. The Old School is perhaps a new school built to replace the one at the Lyceum. This school on Church Drive was built in 1903 as a purpose built establishment following the passing of the Elementary Education Act of 1902. A careful look at the playground shows it to be sunken. This marks the position of another of the tidal inlets which, before Port Sunlight, drained into the River Mersey. At the same time a new church was also built. Christ Church welcomed its first congregation in 1904. There was once a Bridge here and another stream flowed down into the Mersey from a channel situated close to the Bridge Inn. Nearby are a pool and fountain dating from 1913, but the bronze fountain was erected in 1950 as a gift from the trustees of the Lady Lever Art Gallery.

6. **The Lady Lever Art Gallery** (0151 478 4136) Admission free.

(Open daily except Christmas week.) Although the Art Gallery was planned as early as 1913 the First World War prevented its completion until 1922. Here is a collection of splendid Wedgwood ceramics and pre-Raphaelite paintings by Millais, Burne-Jones and Rossetti. There are also British landscapes by Turner and Constable plus portraits by Gainsborough, Romney and Reynolds. Furniture is not neglected either mainly dating from the 18th century. There is also a shop and a very attractive café.

7. This is not just a place for tourists – the area around the fountains overlooks the Art Gallery and is a popular meeting point for local people. Children often paddle in the shallow pond around the fountain. There is a grassy avenue with lots of seats – ideal for a quiet picnic – which leads up to the War Memorial.

8. The War Memorial was designed by Sir William Goscombe John to commemorate the employees of Unilever and villagers who died in two world wars. War Memorials are all moving but occasionally a monument can be regarded as an art form. This is one such monument. Here there is also a memorial to the victims of the Hillsborough football tragedy. From the steps, a sweeping

The fountains and pond in front of the art gallery

Houses at Port Sunlight

panorama reveals the fountain and the Lady Lever Art Gallery plus the grassy areas, which are known locally as the Diamond.

Lord Leverhulme was full of ambition, right up to his death in May 1925. His Christmas card for 1924 had a verse on it which read:

Give me always a goal to try for
Let me do it till my days be spent,
Give me a dream to fight and die for
And I shall be content

As I completed my stroll I reflected on the route. I too am always content to see a ray of Port Sunlight which graces the ancient banks of the Mersey.

From the War Memorial return to the station area passing the Heritage Centre on the left, the Gladstone Theatre on the right.

Footnote

In 2004, Port Sunlight was given a Lottery Grant and a new Heritage Centre will come on line, which will be a fascinating addition.

Walk 26: New Brighton

Directions: Follow the M53 to its end. New Brighton is well signed along the A544. It can also be reached via the Mersey tunnels. There is a large parking area around the old pier and overlooking Perch Rock. This walk can be centred either on the station or this car park.

Public Transport: Reached via Merseyrail (0151 236 7676), this walk could begin from New Brighton Station or from the car park. Those who wish to conclude their journey along the Mersey by exploring both banks may well prefer to use the rail route. New Brighton Bus Station is only two minutes walk from Fort Perch Rock.

Map Reference: OS Explorer 266 & 275 Grid Reference 307 940

Distance: 4 miles

Time: 2 hours

New Brighton seldom gets a mention as a seaside resort. This is a pity, although it did once have a reputation of being a bit 'rough'. Along the shore is a narrow unsafe promenade called Aquarium Parade but perhaps better known as "Ham and Egg Terrace, the favourite resort of the Liverpool and Lancashire Trippers and Roughs". This was written by Sulley in 1889 and nobody grumbled when this "den of iniquity" was demolished in 1906 and replaced by the Victoria Gardens with its Floral Pavilion and Grandstand.

This new century has seen New Brighton enjoy another redevelopment and it now deserves to be placed high on the list of the River Mersey's treasures. Those who visit by car, bus or train should not grumble at our modern transport. I wonder what correspondence would be generated if they were faced with a set of rules given in 1904. When the workers of Bass, Ratcliffe and Gretton's Brewery in Staffordshire visited Liverpool and New Brighton they were told that "It is imperative that all persons should travel both ways by their own train. Changing to other trains, and particularly staying for later trains cannot be allowed. All persons detected breaking this urgent regulation will be left behind ... and the Excursion Ticket will be forfeited".

Isn't modern travel a delight?

The Route

1. In the mid 1990s I was commissioned by Merseytravel and BBC Radio Merseyside to record and write a series of walking guides around Liverpool. This was called Green Hearts. The New Brighton station is an ideal place to begin an exploration of the most under-rated of all the Wakes Resorts in the North West. This route is also an ideal location to enjoy a last stroll along the Wirral bank.

All that was present in what is now New Brighton was a huge complex of sand hills close to the settlement of Wallasey with nothing but panoramic views. This would have been quite enough for most people, but the businessman James Atherton had more ambitious plans. When he retired from business in Liverpool in 1830 he bought 170 acres and set about developing a watering place to attract the rich. He created his New Brighton!

Many unscrupulous folk were skilled in separating people from their hard-earned wages. Sideshows cheated everyone and prostitution, drinking, thieving and brawling became commonplace.

2. **Perch Rock, Lighthouse and Marine Lake.** From the station turn right and along Victoria Road. Pass the car park on the left.

At the turn of the 20th century, the sands here were clean and hard, a delight for children intent upon the building of sand castles. At New Brighton they had a model to copy in the form of Perch Rock battery. This red sandstone fort housed around one hundred thirty-two-pounder Armstrong guns, which guarded the entrance to Liverpool Bay, tel: 0151 630 2707.

The fort was built in 1825, the same year as the lighthouse, which is situated further out to sea. Perch battery only saw active service once and that was during the First World War when it fired at "either a U Boat or a floating log". Neither sank.

The lighthouse replaced Beacon Perch, which charged vessels six pence (2½ new pence) for literally providing a guiding light, which was so vital to negotiate this notoriously difficult channel into Liverpool.

In 1958 the War Office sold the fort, which after a period as a pleasure centre has been restored to something of its original form. Here

Walk 26.
New Brighton

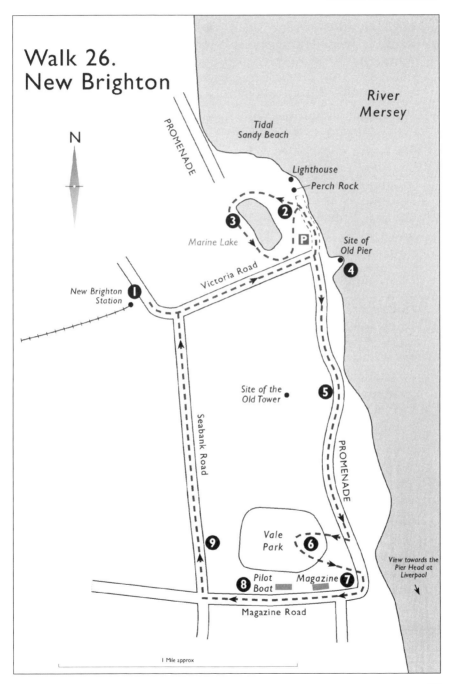

River
Mersey

N

PROMENADE

Tidal
Sandy Beach

Lighthouse

Perch Rock

2

3

Marine Lake

P

Site of
Old Pier

4

Victoria Road

New Brighton
Station

1

Seabank Road

Site of the
Old Tower

5

PROMENADE

Vale
Park

6

9

View towards the
Pier Head at
Liverpool

Pilot
Boat

8

Magazine

7

Magazine Road

1 Mile approx

are exhibitions and a small museum. There are informative displays including aviation, incorporating the "Luftwaffe over Merseyside" and Archaeology. There are also displays of events concerning the *Titanic*, *Listerine* and the submarine HMS *Thetis*, which sank in Liverpool Bay with great loss of life in 1942.

Above the entrance gate is the coat of arms of George IV who was for so long the Prince Regent but who was on the throne when Perch Rock was constructed. The building now has a Grade 2 listing. There are regular events including jazz and band concerts plus military re-enactments. A refreshment room serves tea, coffee and light snacks. On the walls are photographs showing the history of the Blue Funnel Shipping Line and of 'Old' New Brighton.

3. The circular promenade route around the Marine Lake is in an excellent state of repair and there is parking on the front and around Perch Rock. The wonderful views across the bay remain unchanged: look seawards and say goodbye to the Mersey. Next stop America!

4. As Liverpool Docks expanded and large oil refineries mushroomed on the Wirral Bank the New Brighton sands were badly affected. In recent years the resort has spent time and effort on the cleaning up of its environment. The only pity is that the once proud pier has gone forever. This was built in 1885 and remained an important focus until, despite protests from conservationists, it was dismantled in 1973.

It is easy to understand why the pier was removed. The changes in the position of the local sandbanks caused by the expansion of the Seaforth Docks on the opposite bank left New Brighton pier high and dry except on the highest spring tides.

5. This stretch of the Promenade is a car free zone and now regarded as a viewing point for naturalists whatever the state of the tide. Many spend the whole day between Perch Rock and the Promenade enjoying views over Liverpool and listing the wildlife seen. There will be many more visitors over the coming years as Liverpool's skyline changes in response to developments associated with its new status as European City of Culture for 2008.

At high tide on a winter's morning, I watched grey seals, divers, cormorants, common scoters and goldeneyes bobbing and diving

Perch Rock

for food. The rich mud and seaweed encrusted rocks brought grey plover, turnstone, shelduck, curlew and redshank at low water. Summer days mean that sunbathing can be combined with sightings of ringed plover, an assortment of gulls and the occasional herd of adolescent swans.

This also is the place to study the site of the once proud tower. Most commentators in the 1890s pointed out that New Brighton was more vulgar then Blackpool and yet its surrounding scenery was magnificent. The resort had a crying need for an optimistic symbol. In 1897 the idea came – a 621-foot tower, 103 feet higher than Blackpool's. At the time, it was the tallest structure in Britain. The Tower opened in 1900 but for some reason it failed. During the 1914-18 war, the structure became neglected and it was never the success that was anticipated. In 1921 most of the structure was demolished. The theatre and ballroom continued to function until 1961 when both were destroyed by fire. There are signs on the promenade pointing out the location and dimensions of this structure.

6.   Vale Park is well worth exploring and was opened in 1899. The

Victorians can claim to have invented such areas, which served as breathing spaces for working people. There are lovely circular walks around Vale Park and an attractive café is open throughout the year. There are tables set around colourful gardens, which are a delight on warmer days. The Friends of Vale Park ensure that the café is kept open daily and the all-day breakfasts and 'meal deals' for pensioners are popular; tel: 0151 638 2666. The 106 bus from Seacombe Ferry via Liscard stops at the Park Gates.

7. The Promenade at this point changes its name to Magazine Brow. This area was so named because from 1750 the Port of Liverpool needed to store vast amounts of gunpowder to service its warships. A crowded dockland was very vulnerable, so a powder magazine area was constructed among the Wallasey sand dunes. The magazines were embedded in sand, which thus muffled any accidental explosions. As New Brighton developed the new residents were probably less than impressed.

8. There are a number of interesting buildings along the well-named Magazine Road. These read like a history lesson relating to the need for the Mersey to be defended all along the channel leading to the Port of Liverpool.

   There is the Battery House, which used to be called the Liscard Battery. It was built in 1854 and was part of the defence of the estuary in combination with Fort Perch Rock. There is also the Round House that was the base for the magazine's watchmen, who kept an eager eye open for enemy ships or perhaps spies or saboteurs with their eyes on the vulnerable explosives.

   Two pubs also relate to the history of the area. Their names are self-explanatory and they should be visited. The Pilot Boat and the Magazine serve substantial meals and good beer. This is perhaps why it is best to arrive for this stroll on the train!

9. At Seabank Road junction, turn right and return to the station.

SECTION 8: THE LIVERPOOL BANK

There can be no greater contrast between this and the Cheshire bank. Although it is without doubt an urban conurbation there are still splendid walks for those who take the trouble to find them.

Jutting out into the estuary is Hale Point and Lighthouse (see walk 27) and Speke Hall is a half-timbered gem maintained by the National Trust. These two areas are close to the John Lennon (formerly Speke) Airport, and attract an increasing number of tourists (see walk 28).

It comes as something of a surprise to find Liverpool has two rivers, which share an estuary. The Mighty Mersey is obviously well known and is the subject of this and many other books. Few people know that between Liverpool and Formby a smaller watercourse meets the sea. This is the Alt (see walk 29).

Those wishing to conclude their Riverside Rambles along the Mersey to the sea should follow a linear stroll from Otterspool, from the former refuse dump to the Pier Head. Here are museums to celebrate the history of not just the city but also the river. Here then is a fitting place to end the journey and say thank you to one of the world's greatest rivers (see walk 30).

Walk 27: Hale – in search of a Giant and a Child

Directions: Hale is reached via the M6, M58 & M57 or cross the Widnes-Runcorn Bridge and follow the signs for John Lennon (formerly Speke) airport. Hale is 1½ miles from the airport and signed off the A562 between Liverpool and Wigan.

Public Transport: The village is served by a frequent bus service from Liverpool and from Widnes.

Map Reference: OS Explorer 266 & 275 Grid Reference 465 826

Distance: 3½ miles

Time: Allow 2 hours, but naturalists will require much longer.

This stroll around Hale provides expansive views of the mighty Mersey estuary. All estuaries act as a sump with rivers dumping their flow of pollutants. Fortunately the Mersey has had its very own pressure group. The Mersey Estuary Conservation Group (MECG) has worked hard with bodies such as United Utilities, the Environment Agency and the Mersey Basin Campaign to improve water quality. The estuary is recognised as an important bird habitat on a European scale and is regarded as the most important site in Britain for two duck species, the pintail and the teal.

The Mersey has been described as a giant of an estuary but Hale has a very different giant all of its own.

The Route

1. Start at the Childe of Hale pub (0151 425 2954). The first question to be asked along this wonderful stretch of the Mersey estuary is who was the unfortunate Childe who lived from 1578 to 1623? The word child would certainly not satisfy the modern interpretation of the Trades Descriptions Act!

    This giant of a man was 9 feet and 3 inches in height but unlike many "freaks of nature", John Middleton was very strong and agile. He was a renowned wrestler and Sir Gilbert Ireland won many a bet on the outcome of a Middleton contest. In 1617 Sir Gilbert sent

John off to London to
match his giant against the
champion of King James I.
John won easily and the
King gave him an enor-
mous sum of £20 plus a
new suit of clothes. This
was probably a bribe by the
King to persuade this huge
northerner to go home and
leave his own wrestlers
alone! A life-sized portrait
was painted and this now
hangs in Brasenose College
in Oxford. This college has
always attracted large
numbers of Lancastrian
Scholars. A copy of the
painting is exhibited at
Speke Hall (see walk 28).

Hale's giant, carved from a tree

2. From the pub, follow
Church Lane and pass a solid looking thatched cottage. John
Middleton was a big man born in this little house. A small plaque
indicates this birth but care should be taken not to interfere with
the privacy of present-day residents. They have enough distur-
bance these days from the airport flight path. Liverpool's increasing popularity as a tourist location has led to an increase in air
traffic and nowhere is this felt more than at Speke.

3. Continue along the road to St Mary's church on the left. It is a
delight and looks much older than the date of its construction, or
should I say, reconstruction in 1977. This was essential following a
huge fire. There has been a parish church on this site since 1081
and there was a rebuild in 1758. The red sandstone church has an
ancient feel to it, partly because of John Middleton's grave.

There seems to be some confusion about the actual height of John
Middleton. Various authors suggest anything from nine to ten feet.
I can't see a problem however, because a huge inscription on the
grave states nine feet three inches.

I once stood by the grave, watching children who were following the tradition of tossing coins between the metal bars protecting the grave. All they have to do is to toss the coin and make a wish. The money collected contributes to the maintenance of the grave. On the opposite side of the road is a huge carving of the Giant, fashioned from the trunk of a tree.

4. After digesting a huge slice of Mersey history the next stop leads to the lighthouse and the estuary. Follow the path along Lighthouse Lane and bear right to Hale Head and the lighthouse. The lighthouse provides an ideal focus for watching the estuary wildlife and the structure itself has an interesting history.

Any estuary – even such huge expanses as the Mersey – has potential dangers to shipping and marker buoys have, for centuries, been an essential feature of navigation. As ships became larger the dangers increased and, in 1836, a lighthouse was built on Hale Point. The present building dates from 1906 and it operated until more advanced technology led to its closure in 1958. It is now in the grounds of a private dwelling and I regard this as one of the largest and highest garden sheds in the world!

From the footpath there are splendid views of the lighthouse itself as well as the sweep of the estuary and the backdrop of the Welsh Hills. There are places to sit, stare at the views and enjoy a picnic.

Time should be taken to allow the tide to rise and fall. As water levels change, so does the variety of birdlife; different species can also be seen throughout the year. This is therefore a walk for all seasons.

On the ebb there will be waders such as dunlin, knott, curlew, redshank, shelduck and occasionally in winter geese and swans. These feed on the plants and animals on and around the mud flats. At high tide cormorants and ducks dive for invertebrates and fish.

During the filming of a television documentary I took a helicopter flight over the estuary which was seen as clearly as on a map. From this viewpoint the importance of Hale Point as a navigational aid could clearly be seen. Watching migrating birds in flight leads me to believe that they still use the lighthouse as a focal point.

5. Follow a track between a couple of neat footbridges and cross little

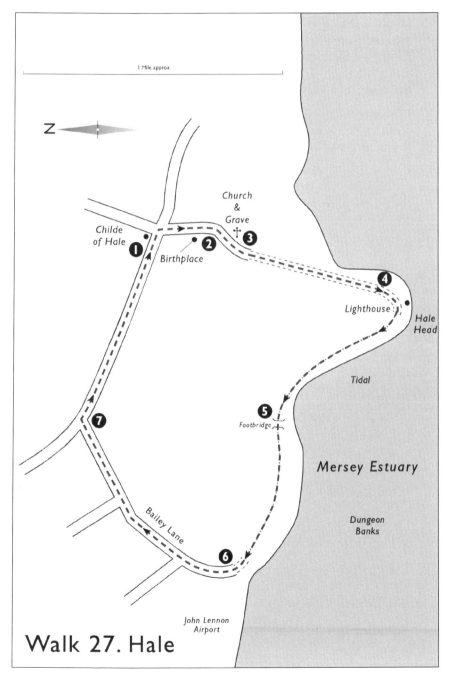

1 Mile approx

N

Childe
of Hale ❶

Birthplace

Church
&
Grave
✝ ❸

❷

❹

Lighthouse

Hale
Head

Tidal

❺
Footbridge

Mersey Estuary

❼

Dungeon
Banks

Bailey Lane

❻

John Lennon
Airport

Walk 27. Hale

streams which are another joy for naturalists. Those in search of spectacular views to right and left will not be disappointed either. There are areas of thistle, which provide food for goldfinch, linnet and stonechat. In winter short-eared owls hunt over the area and there have been recent sightings of barn owls.

Bird watching and botanising in the warmer months mean that walking has to be slow and as quiet as possible. At dawn and dusk there are often sightings of stoat, weasel and red fox.

6. Look out for a set of wooden steps and then continue through fields with houses in the distance. Turn right along Bailey's Lane and return via Hale Road to the Childe of Hale.

Walk 28: Around Speke Hall

Directions: Speke is 8 miles south-east of Liverpool and adjacent to John Lennon Airport. Follow the A561, which links Liverpool and Widnes and turn onto a minor road, with the hall indicated by a brown sign. Pass an entry box, which leads to the extensive car park. The parking fee can be reclaimed when paying for entry to Speke Hall and/or the gardens.

Public Transport: There are railway stations at Hunt's Cross and Garston, which are both around two miles from the hall. There are plenty of buses. For details ring 0151 236 7676.

Speke Hall car park is the starting point for regular summer season mini-bus tours to the old homes of the Beatles John Lennon and Sir Paul McCartney. It has to be accepted that this unique group is an intrinsic part of Merseyside's history. The National Trust owns the Hall itself and the Beatle houses.

The shop and café are both excellently appointed and the toilets are excellent.

Map Reference: OS Explorer 266 & 275 Grid Reference 420 825

Distance: Around 2½ miles allowing for meanders around the gardens and woodlands.

Time: Those who visit the interior of the Hall and then the walk should allow four hours.

The route followed by this walk is one of the easiest in the book because Speke Hall is self-contained. It cannot be missed, however, because it follows footpaths through the only substantial area of woodland remaining on this bank of the Mersey.

Speke Hall itself is one of the best-preserved half-timbered buildings in England. The opening times are: 22 March to 31 October, Wednesday to Sunday 13.00 to 17.30 hrs; 1st November to the first week in December, weekends 13.00 to 16.30 hrs. Tel: 0151 427 7231; Information line 08457 585702 (local rates).

The Route

1. The car park is overlooked by fencing and high screening 'bunds' which have been constructed to isolate the increasingly large complex of John Lennon International Airport.

Speke Hall, with the old moat to the left

2. From the car park head towards a complex of buildings that make up what was once called the Home Farm. Here are the ticket office, shop, café and toilets. Home farm was built in 1885 as a replacement for an earlier complex, which provided food for the family and estate workers. Most large estates were almost entirely self-sufficient and the associated farms like those of monastic houses had to be carefully managed.

    Speke Hall's Home Farm was described as a model unit and it retains much of this atmosphere. There were once cowsheds, stables, pigsties, a blacksmith's shop and a granary. The National Trust now makes good use of the buildings, which continued to function as a farm until the 1940s. The restored 19th-century farm steam engine operates frequently during the season and especially at weekends.

3. From the Home Farm complex follow the signs to the hall and pass the Education rooms and another set of toilets on the left. Continue straight ahead and then turn sharp left to reach the Hall and Gardens.

4. The Hall was built by the Norris family in 1490 using a site that had been a wooded valley not far from the then fishing village of Liver-

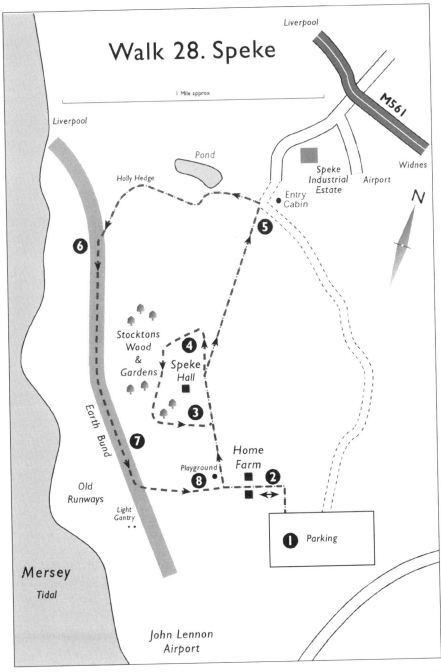

Walk 28. Speke

Liverpool

M561

I Mile approx

Liverpool

Pond

Holly Hedge

Widnes

Speke Industrial Estate

Airport

Entry Cabin

5

N

6

Stocktons Wood & Gardens

4

Speke Hall

3

Earth Bund

7

Old Runways

Home Farm

Playground

8

2

Light Gantry

1 Parking

Mersey

Tidal

John Lennon Airport

159

pool. The grounds of Speke led down to the banks of the River Mersey, now occupied by the airport. The construction of the Hall must have involved the clearing of lots of small trees. The term 'Speke' is Old English for 'brushwood'.

By 1612 the Hall had been extended to include a central courtyard leading into a Tudor Great Hall. The family was wealthy enough to be able to build a protective moat, the outline of which is still very clear – although it is now dry. Inside they also funded ornately decorated plaster ceilings and oak carvings.

The Norris family were ardent Catholics; they supported Charles I against Parliament and were ardent Jacobites in opposition to the Hanoverians. This accounts for the number of cunningly concealed priestholes, which are pointed out on tours of the house. The guides are often dressed in Tudor costume.

Despite their political intrigues the Norris family survived until 1731 when they ran out of male heirs. Speke passed by marriage into the Beauclerk family but they seem to have had little love for the estate. By 1797 Speke was almost derelict. It was then purchased by William Watt, a Liverpool shipping merchant who lavished both time and money on Speke. The Watts family continued in residence until 1921 when Adelaide the last in the Watt line gave the estate to the Norris family. Thus, the history of Speke came full circle.

In 1943, as Liverpool was licking its wounds from the German bombing, Speke passed into the hands of the National Trust and the estate has been well-cared-for ever since.

This walk continues by following the perimeter of the house, keeping this to the left and passing through the splendid garden.

5. At the completion of the circle continue ahead towards the entrance hut. Pass through one metal gate and then turn left through another gate and into what has been called the Sunken Lane. There are views of the Hall to the left and a pond to the right, which is a place to watch waterfowl in the winter. Pass between high hedges mainly composed of holly.

6. Ascend onto a bund of land built to protect the Liverpool airport complex. The path follows the top of the bund, where there are

strategically placed seats. These overlook the airport to the left whilst straight ahead and to the right is the Mersey estuary. Away in the distance are the Welsh hills and the Wirral peninsula. Gorse seems to bloom here during every month of the year and the bushes are attractive to breeding stonechats. Down to the left is Stockton Wood, which was extensively planted in the 19th century to provide cover for game. In medieval times, however, the whole site was wooded.

7. Continue along the bund, which leads to ever-closer views of the airport, developing very quickly and providing a real contrast to the rural tranquillity of the Speke estate. Although Liverpool's is a developing airport it is certainly not new. Indeed Speke was among the first to be established in England. The concept was initiated in 1928 and the first commercial flight took to the air in 1930. On 1st July 1933 the opening ceremony took place. A major reason for choosing this site was that Liverpool has fewer days of fog than many other airports.

8. From the banking descend and turn left through the children's playground and back to the Home Farm complex and the car park.

Walk 29: The Alt Estuary at Hightown

Directions: Follow the A565 Coastal Road from Southport towards Liverpool. Look out for the B5193 signed Hightown to the right. There is adequate parking around the village and at the Hightown Hotel. From the Hightown hotel go into the village centre. At the War Memorial there is a sign to the Alt Centre. There is limited parking by the boat yard.

Public Transport: There is a regular rail service between Liverpool and Southport with Hightown and Hall Road stations ideal locations for this linear walk.

Map Reference: OS Explorer 275 & 285 Grid Reference 301 035

Distance: 3 miles linear. This is why the two stations are ideal, but there is so much to see in this estuarine area that I usually prefer to retrace my steps especially in the summer. There is also a wide selection of marked tracks available through the dunes.

Time: Allow 2 hours for the 3 miles

The River Alt is very rarely mentioned and few students of the Mersey even know where it is. It is a slow flowing river running through Knowsley and Liverpool and is therefore Liverpool's second river.

The Alt and its little tributary streams make up around 48 miles (75kms) of urbanised watercourse. Its recent history has not been a happy one and its banks have been straightened, deepened and even culverted over much of its course.

The Alt was heavily polluted by urban run-off, but the Environment Agency has recently been involved in an impressive rehabilitation scheme, which is set to continue for some years yet. As part of the Mersey Basin Campaign a number of River Valley Initiatives were set up. These continue to thrive and one of these is focussed on the River Alt. An officer works full-time, helping to promote the river improvements. Regular meetings are held with United Utilities, the Environment Agency and other stakeholders concerned with the welfare of the Alt.

Launching a boat on the Alt

Those requiring more detailed information than is contained in this walk should make contact with these five hard-working organisations:

⊜ The Sefton Coast and Countryside Source: 01704 570173

⊜ The RSPB: 01704 536378

⊜ English Nature: 01704 578774

⊜ The National Trust: 01704 878591

⊜ The Mersey Basin Campaign: 0161 242 8200

Obviously, flood defence in this sensitive area has to be of major importance here and planners have divided the 15-mile length of the Alt into two. The Upper Alt flows through Huyton, Knowsley, Kirkby, Aughton, Maghull and Aintree but the flood risk is not high compared with that of the Lower Alt. This covers the area from Maghull to the coastline between Crosby and Ainsdale. For this area a flood defence plan is being developed and is due to deliver a report in the summer of 2005. Indications so far would seem to suggest that a development of controlled wetlands will benefit wildlife and those who enjoy studying the fauna and flora.

The Route

Hightown

1. From the railway station find the Hightown Hotel, which has a bowling green and one of the most varied menus to be found in the area. This remains open every day. In the summer is an outdoor area but families are welcomed at all times. Follow first Alt Road, then Lower Alt Road and past a roundabout. Pass the War Memorial and then down to the river. The Alt centre is signed.

2. The river here is a perfect spot to watch birds – especially in winter, when many dunlin roost on the marshy areas and find lots of food in the mud. Their diet consists of invertebrates, which now thrive thanks to low pollution levels.

   Other winter waders found here include redshank, curlew, lapwing and bar-tailed godwit. Wildfowl are numerous including shelduck, teal, wigeon, pintail. Most birds seem to ignore the sound of gunfire, which is frequent during daylight hours. The birds seem to know that Altcar Rifle Range is a training area for military marksmen and women and is not directed at them. As the marshlands develop hereabouts it is hoped that avocets, which are occasionally seen in the area, may eventually breed.

3. From the river estuary area follow a gravel path above the river. If you have already heard shooting look out for a red flag, which indicates that members of the Territorial Army are at practice. Follow a path bearing left away from the river. This is on the line of the Sefton Coastal Path. This path has gradually developed and the summer of 2003 saw a determined effort to publicise the walk, which runs from Southport towards Liverpool. Copies of the Guide can be obtained from the Southport Tourist Information Centre or from the Ainsdale Discovery Centre (01704 533333).

   At this point a short diversion down to the river close to a Sailing Club is well worth the time especially at low tide. There seem to be a number of 'rocks' strewn with seaweed in the estuarine mud. Actually this is what remains of an ancient forest swamped thousands of years ago when sea levels increased.

4. The path now leads through an impressive dune system and marker posts indicate the main route. Winter walkers will find plenty of birds to see including rarities such as merlin and

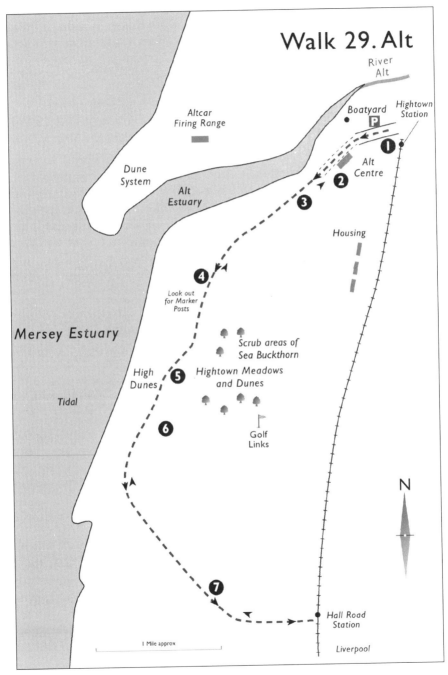

Walk 29. Alt

River Alt

Altcar Firing Range

Boatyard

Hightown Station

Dune System

Alt Estuary

Alt Centre

Housing

Look out for Marker Posts

Mersey Estuary

Scrub areas of Sea Buckthorn

High Dunes

Hightown Meadows and Dunes

Tidal

Golf Links

N

Hall Road Station

Liverpool

1 Mile approx

short-eared owl. Summer strollers will find dune flowers such as heartsease pansy, birds foot trefoil, rest harrow and in damp spots there will be several orchid species.

There are two real rarities on the Schedule 1 protection list. These are the Natterjack toad and it is hoped that the Sand Lizard may extend its range here from Formby. Here is also an excellent place to watch butterflies.

In the autumn Evening Primrose grows in profusion. This was introduced by accident from America. Because cotton was so light, soil was carried in ships to act as ballast. When this ballast was emptied at Liverpool, the seeds of plants including the Evening Primrose germinated which has thrived ever since. The plant is not a primrose but the flowers are the same shade of yellow and they also open in the evening and hence the name. The American Indians used extracts of Evening Primrose to ease the problems associated with childbirth and women still make use of the oil from the plant.

5. Apart from the obvious sand dunes there are some 'bumps' in this area that need explaining. When Liverpool was bombed during World War II huge areas of rubble had to be removed and some was taken to Hightown. Now grassed over, the Hightown meadows are a botanical delight and an unexpected gift from the horrors of conflict.

6. Pass the golf links on the left. The path first veers seawards and then left towards the West Lancashire Golf club. There are many internationally famous courses in this area including Birkdale. All links courses (seaside areas) are tricky with sandy fairways and winds sweeping in off the sea. The areas surrounding these courses are all full with fauna and flora.

7. Pass the Coastguard building and, then, if you want to shorten the walk, turn left down Hall Road West and on to Hall Road station.

Those who retrace their steps should remember that there are many alternative routes through the dunes, which will reveal ever more wildlife. I have followed this route in all weathers and all seasons and a look at my diaries clearly shows that the inward and outward routes are always different. The six-mile circular, therefore, is worth the extra effort.

Walk 30: Otterspool to the Pier Head

Directions: Follow the A5036 which runs between Liverpool and Widnes and parallel with the Mersey. Coming from the Speke area a left turn along Jericho Lane leads to a small car park. Further on another left turn leads to Otterspool Park. There is lots of parking here. The Otters Pool pub is the perfect base for this stroll. There is also plenty of free parking on the Albert Dock but it can be busier than Otterspool.

A massive building programme around the Albert Dock relating to Liverpool's European City of Culture status for 2008 means that it is better to start the walk from Otterspool.

Public Transport: By far the best way to explore this area is to arrive by train.

Map Reference: OS Explorer 266 & 275 Grid Reference 375 859

Distance: 3 miles linear.

Time: Hard to estimate because there are so many bars, coffee shops, restaurants, shops and museums.

The poet John Masefield (1878-1967) was a mariner in the days of sail and he wrote these words:

A wind's in the heart of me, a fire's in my heels
I am tired of brick and stone and rumbling wagon wheels
I hunger for the sea's edge, the limits of the land
Where the wild old Atlantic is shouting at the sand

I am very much a landlubber but as I completed the last of my River Rambles I shared the poet's feelings.

The Route

1. Otterspool Park and Promenade is often a mass of flowers and well-cut grass, and is a bright and breezy walk along the river. Here is a perfect example of what a city can do with its rubbish if it sets its mind to it.

Until the 1930s, a tidal path was treacherous because of the mud and seaweed. Until the 19th century, Otterspool was just that – a common haunt of what is now one of our rarest mammals.

Later came the plans for the first Mersey Tunnel. What was to be done with all the rock? In 1932 the council constructed retaining walls alongside the river and then dumped the tunnel rock and domestic refuse, which solved two problems at once. Then came the Second World War when German bombers wrecked the city and debris was dumped at Otterspool and other areas such as Hightown. After the war the scheme continued and, in 1950, the first stretch of Otterspool promenade was opened to the public.

2. This really is a walk through history but alas, there are still a couple of black spots. Although the riverside promenade leads directly to Pier Head, a small area of land is Government-owned as a Customs and Excise area. Occasionally the route is closed and walkers have to divert onto the A5036 and then return to the Promenade.

To the right is the site of the Liverpool International Garden Festival. This is now derelict and what an expensive flop this has been. I was present at the opening and the area was full of colour and the entertainment was wonderful. Keep walking alongside this site, however, because things are set to improve.

The Garden Festival of 1984 was the largest event to take place since the Festival of Britain in 1951. 250 acres of derelict land was

Shanty singers at the International Garden Festival, 1984

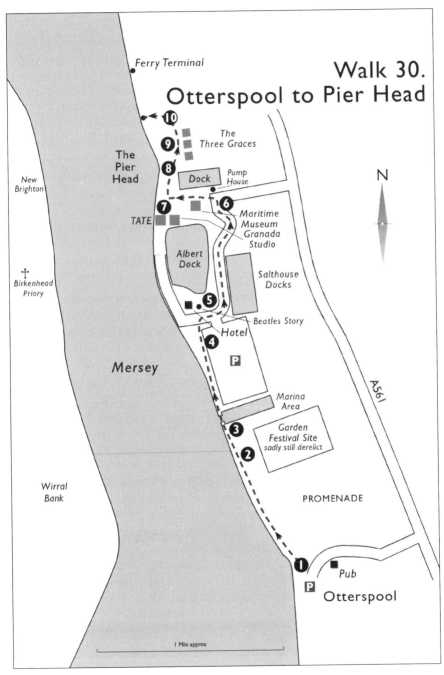

Walk 30.
Otterspool to Pier Head

Ferry Terminal

The Three Graces

The Pier Head

New Brighton

N

Dock

Pump House

TATE

Maritime Museum
Granada Studio

Albert Dock

Birkenhead Priory

Salthouse Docks

Beatles Story

Hotel

P

Mersey

Marina Area

A561

Garden Festival Site
sadly still derelict

Wirral Bank

PROMENADE

Pub

Otterspool

I Mile approx

landscaped at enormous cost. In the space of six weeks 600,000 tons of silt from the disused Herculaneum Dock and 1.5 million tons of sand produced an area capable of parking 10,000 cars. An out-of-date oil terminal complete with an underground tank and two large jetties were removed and the rubble used to help landscape slopes. Tree planting was a major enterprise and so was the Festival Hall destined to become a major Sports and Leisure Centre.

Throughout the 1980s and early 1990s, Liverpool was not a happy city and to say that the Garden Festival site fell into disrepair is an understatement. These scars will be healed as developments associated with Liverpool's status as European Capital of Culture comes on line by 2008.

3. The seats along the Promenade are ideal picnic spots with views over the Mersey and its wildlife. Water quality is now high enough to support lots of fish, invertebrates and the occasional salmon plus regular sightings of grey seal and even a bottlenose dolphin!

In 1984, Michael Heseltine visited the Toxteth area and said that the state of the Mersey was "an affront to a civilised society". This led directly to the setting up of the Mersey Basin Campaign. The Mersey without doubt is becoming a major tourist location and the cleaner the river water the more attractive it will become.

4. Follow the promenade past the impressive marina and car parks on the right. Bear right and cross a roofed bridge, leading directly to the Beatles Story Museum, which attracts thousands of fans and those who are simply curious about the Fab Four. Here is the Cavern Club and directions on how to find Sir Paul McCartney's former home, now owned by the National Trust. Details of John Lennon's origins are also within easy reach (see walk 28).

5. Turn right at the Beatles Story Museum and then immediate left. On the left are shops, bars and commercial premises. Salthouse Dock is on the right and to the left, seen through gaps in buildings, is Albert Dock, one of the most important maritime complexes anywhere in the world. The huge former warehouses surrounding the dock make up the largest Grade I listed buildings in the country and the Tourist Information Centre is an ideal place to buy memorabilia and literature concerned with Liverpool and Merseyside.

Opened by Prince Albert in 1846 the Dock was designed by Jesse Hartley and his aim was to accommodate the largest sailing ships in

Albert Dock

the world. As steam replaced sail and the size of vessels increased the Albert Dock was largely redundant. In 1972 it closed and it was not until 1984 that a spectacular restoration was opened to visitors. The best way to appreciate the dock is to take a trip on a little ferry-boat, which tours the complex. One of these vessels is amphibious and tours the pathways around the docklands.

6. Keep the Dock on the left and find the Granada TV Studio with a pub called the Pumphouse Inn in front. There are few television buildings as impressive as Granada's Newsroom, which is based in the Old Custom's House. The pillared entrance has a classical look to it. The Pump House (0151 709 2367), which formerly controlled water levels, now provides food and drink to visitors. There are tables outside the Inn and it is a popular eating area overlooked by the three Pier Head buildings.

7. The Maritime Museum is found by turning left between the Granada TV studio and the Pumphouse Inn. The museum (entry is free) is the place to celebrate the history of the city. This is why a whole day should be devoted to this walk.

The Maritime Museum and the Museum of Liverpool Life play a vital role in the portrayal of one of the world's great maritime cities.

Here too is the Western Approaches Exhibition, which recreates a labyrinth of tunnels, and rooms, which were the Chief of Staff Headquarters during the Battle of the Atlantic in World War II.

8. From the Maritime Museum look straight ahead at the Pier Head. There are usually sailing ships tied up which provide a uniquely beautiful atmosphere. Turn left and cross a bridge. Ahead is the Promenade with views over to Birkenhead, Wallasey and New Brighton. There are many seats overlooking the river but this route bears right and onto the Pier Head. To the left, however, is the Northern Branch of the Tate Gallery.

9. The Pier Head and the Three Graces, which dominate it, relate not to the age of sail but to that of the transatlantic liner. The granite-faced Royal Liver Building dates between 1908 and 1911. It was the first building in the world to be built of reinforced concrete. On top are the famous Liver Birds and close to the top is the largest clock face in Britain. Built in 1907, the Port of Liverpool Building is surmounted by a green dome supported on pillars, which gives it a distinctive Venetian feel.

The 'third Grace' is the Cunard Building constructed during the First World War and it was from here that the Cunard Company ran its transatlantic business, which only declined with the coming of air traffic.

10. From the Three Graces, continue to complete this journey at the Ferry Terminal (0151 474 4444). By far the best way to conclude this walking portrait of the Mersey is to put your feet up and take a pleasure trip on a Mersey Ferry. You may well hear Jerry Marsden's tune 'Ferry across the Mersey' echoing out across the water. Sail away towards the Ship Canal and think about the rowboat ferry at Thelwall (see walk 19) and also the Eastham Ferry (walk 24). The monks also played their part in carrying passengers over the river. The monks at Norton Priory (walk 12) also played a part as did the brethren at Birkenhead Priory, which is well worth a visit.

Footnote

This is a reminder that, having covered 30 walks, I have still not scratched the surface of the history of this wonderful river. A good excuse to return?

Further Reading

Altcar - The Story of a Rifle Range The Territotial Army, 1989

Anderson, P. *Tame Valley Wildlife* Greater Manchester Council, 1981

Bracegirdle, C. *The Dark River – The Irwell* Sherratt, 1971

Corbett, J. *The River Irwell* Abel Heywood, 1907

Davies, G.E. & A.R. *The River Irwell and its Tributaries* John Heywood, 1890

Falk, B. *The Bridgewater Millions* Hutchinson, 1942

Freethy, R. *The River Mersey* Terence Dalton, 1985

Greenwood, E.F. (Ed) *Ecology and Landscape Development of the Mersey Basin* Liverpool University Press, 1996

Greenwood , W. *The County Book – Lancashire* Robert Hale, 1951

Palmer, W.T. *The River Mersey* Robert Hale, 1944

Also of interest:

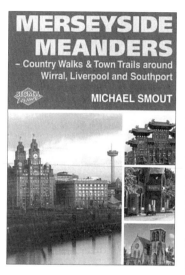

MERSEYSIDE MEANDERS: Country Walks & Town Trails around Wirral, Liverpool and Southport

Michael Smout

Here are 31 walks to celebrate the pleasures of walking in the Merseyside area. A few are city walks, but most are through open land, fields or coastline. There are no mountains or hills and all of the walks are 'easy' – hence the title. Many well-known places are featured, including Liverpool, Aintree, Halewood and Southport – but such gems as Port Sunlight, Thurstaston and Ness also await you with their fascinating heritage, history and ecological interest. £7.95

WATERSIDE WALKS IN THE LAKE DISTRICT

Colin Shelbourn

A unique compilation of 25 walks around and alongside a selection of the many water features to be found in this favourite walking area – lakes, tarns, becks, rivers and waterfalls. Ranging from 1 to 16km, from gentle strolls to more strenuous hikes there are suitable walks for all age groups. Each walk includes information about parking, the length of the walk, a clear map to guide you, the level of difficulty, some very interesting facts of particular relevance and many beautiful photographs. £7.95

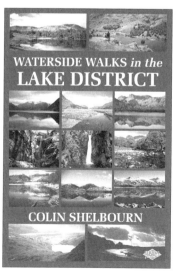